# Homophobia: A Weapon of Sexism

# Homophobia:
# A Weapon of Sexism

## Suzanne Pharr

*Illustrations by Susan G. Raymond*

**Chardon Press**

2  3  4  5  6  2002  2001  2000

Cover design by Deborah Dudley
Back cover photo by Rebecca G. Carey
Book design by Robert Cooney
Typeset in Century Text by Judy Lambert

Published by Chardon Press
Berkeley, California

Distributed by the Women's Project
2224 Main Street
Little Rock, AR 72206
phone 501-372-5113/fax 501-372-0009

Library of Congress Catalog Card No.: 97-68239
ISBN 1-890759-01-5

*Dedicated to women everywhere who seek freedom.*
*May they find one another and create*
*the movement that transforms the world.*

# ACKNOWLEDGMENTS

This book comes to publication with many friends and supporters. Without them, it would not have been created.

First, I want to thank the hundreds of women who participated in the homophobia workshops and contributed their best political ideas to this analysis. Because of them and their vision of freedom, this book speaks for lesbians everywhere.

Kerry Lobel provided deep sustaining support that was unremitting even when I hesitated before the task. Because of her belief that this work was important, she generously assumed many of my responsibilities so that I would have time to write.

P. Catlin Fullwood was an integral part of the development of this analysis as we worked together in workshops on racism and homophobia. Moreover, she gave me friendship, humor, and always courage to move closer to the truth.

Many friends provided critical readings of the manuscript. In particular, Barbara Smith, Sandra Butler, Eric Rofes and Susan Bonner strengthened the work by their reflections and comments.

And finally, I want to thank Kim Klein, whose support for publishing this book encouraged me to go forward with it, and Nancy Adess, whose careful editing and joyful spirit have made publishing a pleasure.

Suzanne Pharr
Little Rock
*August 1988*

# Introduction

THIS WORK presents a theory about homophobia and sexism that comes out of two major experiences of my life. It is therefore a theory whose methodology is subjective, whose truths are perceived through the repetition and accumulation of experience. It is the theory of both observed and felt truth. It is an analysis that did not come until years of witness had passed and then came slowly, piece by piece like a quilt whose blocks seemed isolated units until finally laid together to show the design.

The theory presented here is about homophobia in general which includes its effect on both lesbians and gay men, but the discussion centers primarily on its effect on heterosexual women and lesbians, the aspect I know most intimately.

One major source of this theory is the battered women's movement. For four years as Co-chair of the Lesbian Task Force of the National Coalition Against Domestic Violence, I presented homophobia workshops to state coalitions and local battered women's programs. These workshops grew from a concern of women in the battered women's movement about the homophobic treatment of lesbian workers as well as about lesbian baiting of domestic violence workers in general. There was also a growing concern about the lack of safe space (physical and psychological safety) for battered lesbians who sought services from battered women's programs.

For two years through the Women's Project I was privileged to be funded by the Chicago Resource Center and the Windom Fund to present two-day homophobia and internalized homophobia workshops for non-lesbians and lesbians in organizations throughout the United States. The general workshop for all women was an analysis of homophobia, why it is every woman's issue, and ways to work against it for the good of all people. The workshop for lesbians on internalized homophobia was an examination of how living in a homophobic world damages lesbians and an analysis of ways we can set ourselves free within this world while working to change it.

When I say I was privileged to be able to do these workshops, the privilege came from several sources. First, I might not have felt safe enough to do them if, like many lesbians, I had had a young child whose custody I would have risked losing if challenged in court; if I had had a family that would have cast me out; or if I had risked losing all reasonable means of making a living. However, I have no children, my family either accepts or tolerates me, and my employment is reasonably secure. Also, I am able to do this work as a middle-aged woman with good health, a moderate income, and above all, white-skinned privilege. I do not risk the additional dangers that lesbians of color face.

Another privilege, which grew greater as workshop added to workshop over the years, has been the opportunity to learn from participants, most of whom were battered women and workers in shelters for battered women. It is not an exaggeration to say that they taught me most of what I know on this subject. It was from listening especially to battered women, women of color and lesbians that I drew the connection between homophobia and violence against women and finally the overall connection to economics and sexism. We have said for a long time in the battered women's movement that all of our truth is found in our stories, and certainly I have found this to be so, for in the stories of battered women I have learned the truth of the interconnectedness of all oppressions and how they are connected to my life as a lesbian.

The other major source of this theory is my own life as a woman whose sexual identity is lesbian. Beginning at fourteen, this identity within a world that hated and feared lesbians led me to live a life of invisibility where I showed the world only a small portion of who I was, and even that portion was a lie, an alienated piece of self that indicated to the world that I did not live with intimate, social connections. Out of fear of loss, I chose a double life, a fragmented self for sixteen years. Not only was I alienated from the world but my internal alienation was extreme and dangerous to my mental health.

Why did I choose such a difficult and painful path? My answer is a variation on a theme of many lesbians' stories. I enjoyed a very healthy childhood on a small dirt farm in Georgia, the youngest of eight children of parents who believed in the value and dignity of hard work, in cleanliness and good food, in regular committed church attendance, and in what Faulkner called the old verities of sympathy, compassion, sacrifice, honesty, and truth. And my sexual identity was outside what was known in this poor farming community. I kept it hidden while I pushed for a place of honor and worth, working my way through college and graduate school to become a university teacher, a profession of respect in my family.

But all along the way, there was the question of who I was, how little or how much of a life I chose to live. Like everyone else, I was a complex human being, and part of this complexity was that in my humanness, I was a sexual being. So I chose as much fullness of life as I could attain without losing those things I cherished so highly: my family, my friends and community, my university job. That is, I acted out of my sexual identity and had a social life that was woman-centered but I lived externally in and lied to a man-centered world. The image I presented to the world was of a woman who was slightly odd and eccentric, mostly a loner, detached from close relationships, asexual, often mysterious, and always very, very serious about work.

To keep my identity safe meant that I had to be constantly

vigilant and lie, primarily through omission but sometimes through commission, virtually every minute of every day. I had to put one large part of myself in exile. The cost was enormous. I could not have authentic friendships because I could not talk about my life. My life could not be shared with my family which in turn necessitated superficial relationships. The stress of maintaining vigilance over the lies I had to create for safety made me never able to relax. Perhaps worst of all was the damage to my sense of self, my sense of integrity. As a woman who had grown up deeply rooted in the church, albeit in tormented debate with it, and as a Southerner with deeply held and mostly unexamined values of courage and honesty, I had to view myself as a woman who lied because of fear.

And yet at the time, the cost seemed worth it. In the 1950s and 1960s, there was no support for lesbian identity within the dominant culture, and since I knew no lesbians other than my partner, I had no lesbian community of support to fall back on. Already feeling in exile and alone, I did not think I could bear losing the connections to the world that I had, especially my family and its supportive community and the job that I had earned at considerable sacrifice.

But never was I easy with the choice I had made to live a life of invisibility, so when support for freedom did arrive, I was more than ready for it. It was after my greatest attempt at exile, a two-year stay in New Zealand, that I moved to New Orleans in 1969 to do graduate work in English and came face to face with the newly reborn women's liberation movement. It was the beginning of massive change for women everywhere, and it was earthshaking for me.

After I had attended two sessions of my first consciousness-raising group which was made up of seven heterosexual women and me, I realized that this experience was one of the most important that had ever happened to me, a time of transformation, and that if I was going to talk about my life, then I had to talk about *my life*, my whole and real life. Nervous and extremely fearful yet excited, I went to the third session and said openly at age 30, for the first time in my life, "I have to tell you something. I am a lesbian." And those good women gave the response that set me on the path to finding my freedom: "Tell us what that is like."

From that moment began the long, careful process of coming out to those I love and those I do not love, of learning to choose the time and place, of learning there are still physical safety issues, of learning—in the end—that there is no substitute for freedom, no matter how hard it is won. There also began the slow understanding of the connection between sexism and homophobia and the beginning of a life commitment to work for freedom for myself, for women—all women—everywhere.

# Homophobia:
# A Weapon of Sexism

HOMOPHOBIA—the irrational fear and hatred of those who love and sexually desire those of the same sex. Though I intimately knew its meaning, the word homophobia was unknown to me until the late 1970s, and when I first heard it, I was struck by how difficult it is to say, what an ugly word it is, equally as ugly as its meaning. Like racism and anti-Semitism, it is a word that calls up images of loss of freedom, verbal and physical violence, death.

In my life I have experienced the effects of homophobia through rejection by friends, threats of loss of employment, and threats upon my life; and I have witnessed far worse things happening to other lesbian and gay people: loss of children,

1

beatings, rape, death. Its power is great enough to keep ten to twenty percent of the population living lives of fear (if their sexual identity is hidden) or lives of danger (if their sexual identity is visible) or both. And its power is great enough to keep the remaining eighty to ninety percent of the population trapped in their own fears.

Long before I had a word to describe the behavior, I was engaged in a search to discover the source of its power, the power to damage and destroy lives. The most common explanations were that to love the same sex was either abnormal (sick) or immoral (sinful).

My exploration of the sickness theory led me to understand that homosexuality is simply a matter of sexual identity, which, along with heterosexual identity, is formed in ways that no one conclusively understands. The American Psychological Association has said that it is no more abnormal to be homosexual than to be lefthanded. It is simply that a certain percentage of the population *is*. It is not healthier to be heterosexual or righthanded. What is unhealthy—and sometimes a source of stress and sickness so great it can lead to suicide—is homophobia, that societal disease that places such negative messages, condemnation, and violence on gay men and lesbians that we have to struggle throughout our lives for self-esteem.

The sin theory is a particularly curious one because it is expressed so often and with such hateful emotion both from the pulpit and from laypeople who rely heavily upon the Bible for evidence. However, there is significant evidence that the approximately eight references to homosexuality in the Bible are frequently read incorrectly, according to Dr. Virginia Ramey Mollenkott in an essay in *Christianity and Crisis*:

> Much of the discrimination against homosexual persons is justified by a common misreading of the Bible. Many English translations of the Bible contain the word homosexual in extremely negative contexts. But the fact is that the word

2

*homosexual* does not occur anywhere in the Bible. No extant text, no manuscript, neither Hebrew nor Greek, Syriac, nor Aramaic, contains the word. The terms *homosexual* and *heterosexual* were not developed in any language until the 1890's, when for the first time the awareness developed that there are people with a lifelong, constitutional orientation toward their own sex. Therefore the use of the word *homosexuality* by certain English Bible translators is an example of the extreme bias that endangers the human and civil rights of homosexual persons. (*pp. 383-4, Nov. 9, 1987*)

Dr. Mollenkott goes on to add that two words in I Corinthians 6:9 and one word in Timothy 1:10 have been used as evidence to damn homosexuals but that well into the 20th century the first of these was understood by everyone to mean masturbation, and the second was known to refer to male prostitutes who were available for hire by either women or men. There are six other Biblical references that are thought by some to refer to homosexuals but each of these is disputed by contemporary scholars. For instance, the sin in the Sodom and Gommorah passage (Genesis 19:1-10) is less about homosexuality than it is about inhospitality and gang rape. The law of hospitality was universally accepted and Lot was struggling to uphold it against what we assume are heterosexual townsmen threatening gang rape to the two male angels in Lot's home. While people dwell on this passage as a condemnation of homosexuality, they bypass what I believe is the central issue or, if you will, *sin*: Lot's offering his two virgin daughters up to the men to be used as they desired for gang rape. Here is a perfectly clear example of devaluing and dehumanizing and violently brutalizing women.

The eight Biblical references (and not a single one by Jesus) to alleged homosexuality are very small indeed when compared to the several hundred references (and many by Jesus) to money and the necessity for justly distributing wealth. Yet few people go on a rampage about the issue of a just economic system, using the Bible as a base.

Finally, I came to understand that homosexuality, heterosexuality, bi-sexuality are *morally neutral*. A particular sexual identity is not an indication of either good or evil. What is important is not the gender of the two people in relationship with each other but the content of that relationship. Does that relationship contain violence, control of one person by the other? Is the relationship a growthful place for the people involved? It is clear that we must hold all relationships, whether opposite sex or same sex, to these standards.

The first workshops that I conducted were an effort to address these two issues, and I assumed that if consciousness could be raised about the invalidity of these two issues then people would stop feeling homophobic and would understand homophobia as a civil rights issue and work against it. The workshops took a high moral road, invoking participants' compassion, understanding, and outrage at injustice.

The eight-hour workshops raised consciousness and increased participants' commitment to work against homophobia as one more oppression in a growing list of recognized oppressions, but I still felt something was missing. I felt there was still too much unaccounted for power in homophobia even after we looked at the sick and sinful theories, at how it feels to be a lesbian in a homophobic world, at why lesbians choose invisibility, at how lesbian existence threatens male dominance. All of the pieces seemed available but we couldn't sew them together into a quilt.

As I conducted more workshops over the years I noticed several important themes that led to the final piecing together:

1) Women began to recognize that economics was a central issue connecting various oppressions;

2) Battered women began talking about how they had been called lesbians by their batterers;

4

3) Both heterosexual and lesbian women said they valued the workshops because in them they were given the rare opportunity to talk about their own sexuality and also about sexism in general.

Around the same time (1985-86), the National Coalition Against Domestic Violence (NCADV) entered into a traumatic relationship with the U.S. Department of Justice (DOJ), requesting a large two-year grant to provide domestic violence training and information nationally. At the time the grant was to be announced, NCADV was attacked by conservative groups such as the Heritage Foundation as a "pro-lesbian, pro-feminist, anti-family" organization. In response to these attacks, the DOJ decided not to award a grant; instead they formulated a "cooperative agreement" that allowed them to monitor and approve all work, and they assured conservative organizations that the work would not be pro-lesbian and anti-family. The major issue between NCADV and the DOJ became whether NCADV would let an outside agency define and control its work, and finally, during never-ending concern from the DOJ about "radical" and "lesbian" issues, the agreement was terminated by NCADV at the end of the first year. Throughout that year, there were endless statements and innuendoes from the DOJ and some members of NCADV's membership about NCADV's lesbian leadership and its alleged concern for only lesbian issues. Many women were damaged by the crossfire, NCADV's work was stopped for a year, and the organization was split from within. It was lesbian baiting at its worst.

As one of NCADV's lesbian leadership during that onslaught of homophobic attacks, I was still giving homophobia workshops around the country, now able to give even more personal witness to the virulence of the hatred and fear of lesbians and gay men within both institutions and individuals. It was a time of pain and often anger for those of us committed to creating a world free of violence, and it was a time of deep distress for those of us under personal attack. However, my mother, like many mothers, had always said, "All things work for the good," and sure enough, it was out of the accumulation of these experiences that the pieces began coming together to make a quilt of our understanding.

On the day that I stopped reacting to attacks and gave my time instead to visioning, this simple germinal question came forth for the workshops: "What will the world be like without homophobia in it—for everyone, female and male, whatever sexual identity?" Simple though the question is, it was at first shocking because those of us who work in the anti-violence movement spend most of our time working with the damaging, negative results of violence and have little time to vision. It is sometimes difficult to create a vision of a world we have never experienced, but without such a vision, we cannot know clearly what we are working toward in our social change work.

From this question, answer led to answer until a whole appeared of our collective making, from one workshop to another.

Here are some of the answers women have given:

• Kids won't be called tomboys or sissies; they'll just be who they are, able to do what they wish.

• People will be able to love anyone, no matter what sex; the issue will simply be whether or not she/he is a good human being, compatible, and loving.

• Affection will be opened up between women and men, women and women, men and men, and it won't be centered on sex; people won't fear being called names if they show affection to someone who isn't a mate or potential mate.

• If affection is opened up, then isolation will be broken down for all of us, especially for those who generally experience little physical affection, such as unmarried old people.

• Women will be able to work whatever jobs we want without being labeled masculine.

• There will be less violence if men do not feel they have to prove and assert their manhood. Their desire to dominate and control will not spill over from the personal to the level of national and international politics and the use of bigger and better weapons to control other countries.

• People will wear whatever clothes they wish, with the priority being comfort rather than the display of femininity or masculinity.

• There will be no gender roles.

It is at this point in the workshops—having imagined a world without homophobia—that the participants see the analysis begin to fall into place. Someone notes that all the things we have been talking about relate to sexual gender roles. It's rather like the beginning of a course in Sexism 101. The next question is "Imagine the world with no sex roles—sexual identity, which may be in flux, but no sexual gender roles."

Further: imagine a world in which opportunity is not determined by gender or race. Just the imagining makes women alive with excitement because it is a vision of freedom, often just glimpsed but always known deep down as truth. Pure joy.

We talk about what it would be like to be born in a world in which there were no expectations or treatment based on gender but instead only the expectation that each child, no matter what race or sex, would be given as many options and possibilities as society could muster. Then we discuss what girls and boys would be like at puberty and beyond if sex role expectations didn't come crashing down on them with girls' achievement levels beginning to decline thereafter; what it would be for women to have the training and options for economic equity with men; what would happen to issues of power and control, and therefore violence, if there were real equality. To have no prescribed sex roles would open the possibility of equality. It is a discussion women find difficult to leave. Freedom calls.

PATRIARCHY—an enforced belief in male dominance and control—is the ideology and sexism the system that holds it in place. The catechism goes like this: Who do gender roles serve? Men and the women who seek power from them. Who suffers from gender roles? Women most completely and men in part. How are gender roles maintained? By the weapons of sexism: economics, violence, homophobia.

Why then don't we ardently pursue ways to eliminate gender roles and therefore sexism? It is my profound belief that all people have a spark in them that yearns for freedom, and the history of the world's atrocities—from the Nazi concentration camps to white dominance in South Africa to the battering of women—is the story of attempts to snuff out that spark. When that spark doesn't move forward to full flame,

8

it is because the weapons designed to control and destroy have wrought such intense damage over time that the spark has been all but extinguished.

Sexism, that system by which women are kept subordinate to men, is kept in place by three powerful weapons designed to cause or threaten women with pain and loss. As stated before, the three are economics, violence, and homophobia. The stories of women battered by men, victims of sexism at its worst, show these three forces converging again and again. When battered women tell why they stayed with a batterer or why they returned to a batterer, over and over they say it was because they could not support themselves and their children financially, they had no skills for jobs, they could not get housing, transportation, medical care for their children. And how were they kept controlled? Through violence and threats of violence, both physical and verbal, so that they feared for their lives and the lives of their children and doubted their own abilities and self-worth. And why were they beaten? Because they were not good enough, were not "real women," were dykes, or because they stood up to him as no "real woman" would. And the male batterer, with societal backing, felt justified, often righteous, in his behavior—for his part in keeping women in their place.

E CONOMICS must be looked at first because many feminists consider it to be the root cause of sexism. Certainly the United Nations study released at the final conference of the International Decade on Women, held in Nairobi, Kenya, in 1985, supports that belief: of the world's population, women do 75% of the work, receive 10% of the pay and own 1% of the property. In the United States it is also supported by the opposition of the government to the idea of comparable worth and pay equity, as expressed by Ronald Reagan who referred

to pay equity as "a joke." Obviously, it is considered a dangerous idea. Men profit not only from women's unpaid work in
the home but from our underpaid work within horizontal female segregation such as clerical workers or upwardly mobile
tokenism in the workplace where a few affirmative action pro-
motions are expected to take care of all women's economic
equality needs. Moreover, they profit from women's bodies
through pornography, prostitution, and international female
sexual slavery. And white men profit from both the labor of
women and of men of color. Forced economic dependency puts
women under male control and severely limits women's options
for self-determination and self-sufficiency.

This truth is borne out by the fact that according to the
National Commission on Working Women, on average, women
of all races working year round earn only 64 cents to every one
dollar a man makes. Also, the U.S. Census Bureau reports that
only 9 percent of working women make over $25,000 a year.
There is fierce opposition to women gaining employment in
the nontraditional job market, that is, those jobs that traditionally employ less than 25 percent women. After a woman
has gained one of these higher paying jobs, she is often faced
with sexual harassment, lesbian baiting, and violence. It is
clear that in the workplace there is an all-out effort to keep
women in traditional roles so that the only jobs we are "qual-
ified" for are the low-paid ones.

Actually, we have to look at economics not only as the root
cause of sexism but also as the underlying, driving force that
keeps all the oppressions in place. In the United States, our
economic system is shaped like a pyramid, with a few people
at the top, primarily white males, being supported by large
numbers of unpaid or low-paid workers at the bottom. When
we look at this pyramid, we begin to understand the major connection between sexism and racism because those groups at
the bottom of the pyramid are women and people of color. We

then begin to understand why there is such a fervent effort to keep those oppressive systems (racism and sexism and all the ways they are manifested) in place to maintain the unpaid and low-paid labor.

Susan DeMarco and Jim Hightower, writing for *Mother Jones*, report that *Forbes* magazine indicated that "the 400 richest families in America last year had an average net worth of $550 million each. These and less than a million other families—roughly one percent of our population—are at the prosperous tip of our society. . . . In 1976, the wealthiest 1 percent of America's families owned 19.2 percent of the nation's total wealth. (This sum of wealth counts all of America's cash, real estate, stocks, bonds, factories, art, personal property, and anything else of financial value.) By 1983, those at this 1 percent tip of our economy owned 34.3 percent of our wealth. . . . *Today, the top 1 percent of Americans possesses more net wealth than the bottom 90 percent.*" (My italics.) (*May, 1988, pp. 32-33*)

In order for this top-heavy system of economic inequity to maintain itself, the 90 percent on the bottom must keep supplying cheap labor. A very complex, intricate system of institutionalized oppressions is necessary to maintain the status quo so that the vast majority will not demand its fair share of wealth and resources and bring the system down. Every institution—schools, banks, churches, government, courts, media, etc—as well as individuals must be enlisted in the campaign to maintain such a system of gross inequity.

What would happen if women gained the earning opportunities and power that men have? What would happen if these opportunities were distributed equitably, no matter what sex one was, no matter what race one was born into, and no matter where one lived? What if educational and training opportunities were equal? Would women spend most of our youth preparing for marriage? Would marriage be based on economic survival for women? What would happen to issues of power and control? Would women stay with our batterers? If a woman had economic independence in a society where women had equal opportunities, would she still be thought of as owned by her father or husband?

Economics is the great controller in both sexism and racism. If a person can't acquire food, shelter, and clothing and provide them for children, then that person can be forced to do many things in order to survive. The major tactic, worldwide, is to provide unrecompensed or inadequately recompensed labor for the benefit of those who control wealth. Hence, we see women performing unpaid labor in the home or filling low-paid jobs, and we see people of color in the lowest-paid jobs available.

The method is complex: limit educational and training opportunities for women and for people of color and then withhold adequate paying jobs with the excuse that people of color and women are incapable of filling them. Blame the economic victim and keep the victim's self-esteem low through invisibility and distortion within the media and education. Allow a few people of color and women to succeed among the profit-makers so that blaming those who don't "make it" can be intensified. Encourage those few who succeed in gaining power now to turn against those who remain behind rather than to use their resources to make change for all. Maintain the myth of scarcity—that there are not enough jobs, resources, etc., to go around—among the middleclass so that they will not unite with laborers, immigrants, and the unemployed. The method keeps in place a system of control and profit by a few and a constant source of cheap labor to maintain it.

If anyone steps out of line, take her/his job away. Let homelessness and hunger do their work. The economic weapon works. And we end up saying, "I would do this or that—be openly who I am, speak out against injustice, work for civil rights, join a labor union, go to a political march, etc.—if I didn't have this job. I can't afford to lose it." We stay in an abusive situation because we see no other way to survive.

In the battered women's movement abusive relationships are said to be about power and control and the way out of them is through looking at the ways power and control work in our lives, developing support, improving self-esteem, and achieving control over our decisions and lives. We have yet to apply these methods successfully to our economic lives. Though requiring massive change, the way there also lies open for equality and wholeness. But the effort will require at least as much individual courage and risk and group support as it does for a battered woman to leave her batterer, and that requirement is very large indeed. Yet battered women find the courage to leave their batterers every day. They walk right into the unknown. To break away from economic domination and control will require a movement made up of individuals who possess this courage and ability to take risks.

VIOLENCE is the second means of keeping women in line, in a narrowly defined place and role. First, there is the physical violence of battering, rape, and incest. Often when battered women come to shelters and talk about their lives, they tell stories of being not only physically beaten but also raped and their children subjected to incest. Work in the women's anti-violence movement during almost two decades has provided significant evidence that each of these acts, including rape and incest, is an attempt to seek power over and control of another person. In each case, the victim is viewed as an object and is used to meet the abuser's needs. The violence is used to wreak punishment and to demand compliance or obedience.

Violence against women is directly related to the condition of women in a society that refuses us equal pay, equal access to resources, and equal status with males. From this condition comes men's confirmation of their sense of ownership of women, power over women, and assumed right to control women for their own means. Men physically and emotionally abuse women because they *can*, because they live in a world that gives them permission. Male violence is fed by their sense of their *right* to dominate and control, and their sense of superiority over a group of people who, because of gender, they consider inferior to them.

It is not just the violence but the threat of violence that controls our lives. Because the burden of responsibility has been placed so often on the potential victim, as women we have curtailed our freedom in order to protect ourselves from violence. Because of the threat of rapists, we stay on alert, being careful not to walk in isolated places, being careful where we park our cars, adding incredible security measures to our homes —massive locks, lights, alarms, if we can afford them—and we avoid places where we will appear vulnerable or unprotected while the abuser walks with freedom. Fear, often now so commonplace that it is unacknowledged, shapes our lives, reducing our freedom.

As Bernice Reagan of the musical group Sweet Honey in the Rock said at the 1982 National Coalition Against Domestic Violence conference, women seem to carry a genetic memory that women were once burned as witches when we stepped out of line. To this day, mothers pass on to their daughters word of the dangers they face and teach them the ways they must limit their lives in order to survive.

Part of the way sexism stays in place is the societal promise of survival, false and unfulfilled as it is, that women will not suffer violence if we attach ourselves to a man to protect us. A woman without a man is told she is vulnerable to external violence and, worse, that there is something wrong with her. When the male abuser calls a woman a lesbian, he is not so much labeling her a woman who loves women as he is warning her that by resisting him, she is choosing to be outside society's protection from male institutions and therefore from wide-ranging, unspecified, ever-present violence. When she seeks assistance from woman friends or a battered women's shelter, he recognizes the power in woman bonding and fears loss of her servitude and loyalty: the potential loss of his control. The concern is not affectional/sexual identity: the concern is disloyalty and the threat is violence.

The threat of violence against women who step out of line or who are disloyal is made all the more powerful by the fact that women do not have to do anything—they may be paragons of virtue and subservience—to receive violence against our lives: the violence still comes. It comes because of the woman-hating that exists throughout society. Chance plays a larger part than virtue in keeping women safe. Hence, with violence always a threat to us, women can never feel completely secure and confident. Our sense of safety is always fragile and tenuous.

Many women say that verbal violence causes more harm than physical violence because it damages self-esteem so deeply. Women have not wanted to hear battered women say that the verbal abuse was as hurtful as the physical abuse: to acknowledge that truth would be tantamount to acknowledging that *virtually every woman is a battered woman*. It is difficult to keep strong against accusations of being a bitch, stupid, inferior, etc., etc. It is especially difficult when these individual assaults are backed up by a society that shows women in textbooks, advertising, TV programs, movies, etc., as debased, silly, inferior, and sexually objectifed, and a society that gives tacit approval to pornography. When we internalize these messages, we call the result "low self-esteem," a therapeutic individualized term. It seems to me we should use the more political expression: when we internalize these messages, we experience *internalized sexism*, and we experience it in common with all women living in a sexist world. The violence against us is supported by a society in which woman-hating is deeply imbedded.

In "Eyes on the Prize," a 1987 Public Television documentary about the Civil Rights Movement, an older white woman says about her youth in the South that it was difficult to be anything different from what was around her when there was no vision for another way to be. Our society presents images of women that say it is appropriate to commit violence against us. Violence is committed against women because we are seen as inferior in status and in worth. It has been the work of the women's movement to present a vision of another way to be.

Every time a woman gains the strength to resist and leave her abuser, we are given a model of the importance of stepping out of line, of moving toward freedom. And we all gain strength when she says to violence, "Never again!" Thousands of women in the last fifteen years have resisted their abusers to come to this country's 1100 battered women's shelters. There they have sat down with other women to share their stories, to discover that their stories again and again are the same, to develop an analysis that shows that violence is a statement about power and control, and to understand how sexism creates the climate for male violence. Those brave women are now a part of a movement that gives hope for another way to live in equality and peace.


HOMOPHOBIA works effectively as a weapon of sexism because it is joined with a powerful arm, heterosexism. Heterosexism creates the climate for homophobia with its assumption that the world is and must be heterosexual and its display of power and privilege as the norm. Heterosexism is the systemic display of homophobia in the institutions of society. Heterosexism and homophobia work together to enforce compulsory heterosexuality and that bastion of patriarchal power, the nuclear family. The central focus of the rightwing attack against women's liberation is that women's equality, women's self-determination, women's control of our own bodies and lives will damage what they see as the crucial societal institution, the nuclear family. The attack has been led by fundamentalist ministers across the country. The two areas they have focused on most consistently are abortion and homosexuality, and their passion has led them to bomb women's clinics and to recommend deprogramming for homosexuals and establishing camps to quarantine people with AIDS. To resist marriage and/or heterosexuality is to risk severe punishment and loss.

It is not by chance that when children approach puberty and increased sexual awareness they begin to taunt each other by calling these names: "queer," "faggot," "pervert." It is at puberty that the full force of society's pressure to conform to heterosexuality and prepare for marriage is brought to bear. Children know what we have taught them, and we have given clear messages that those who deviate from standard expectations are to be made to get back in line. The best controlling tactic at puberty is to be treated as an outsider, to be ostracized at a time when it feels most vital to be accepted. Those who are different must be made to suffer loss. It is also at puberty that misogyny begins to be more apparent, and girls are pressured to conform to societal norms that do not permit them to realize their full potential. It is at this time that their academic achievements begin to decrease as they are coerced into compulsory heterosexuality and trained for dependency upon a man, that is, for economic survival.

There was a time when the two most condemning accusations against a woman meant to ostracize and disempower her were "whore" and "lesbian." The sexual revolution and changing attitudes about heterosexual behavior may have led to some lessening of the power of the word *whore*, though it still has strength as a threat to sexual property and prostitutes are stigmatized and abused. However, the word *lesbian* is still fully charged and carries with it the full threat of loss of power and privilege, the threat of being cut asunder, abandoned, and left outside society's protection.

To be a lesbian is to be *perceived* as someone who has stepped out of line, who has moved out of sexual/economic dependence on a male, who is woman-identified. A lesbian is perceived as someone who can live without a man, and who is therefore (however illogically) against men. A lesbian is perceived as being outside the acceptable, routinized order of things. She is seen as someone who has no societal institutions to protect her and who is not privileged to the protection of individual males. Many heterosexual women see her as someone who stands in contradiction to the sacrifices they have made to conform to compulsory heterosexuality. A lesbian is perceived as a threat to the nuclear family, to male dominance and control, to the very heart of sexism.

Gay men are perceived also as a threat to male dominance and control, and the homophobia expressed against them has the same roots in sexism as does homophobia against lesbians. Visible gay men are the objects of extreme hatred and fear by heterosexual men because their breaking ranks with male heterosexual solidarity is seen as a damaging rent in the very fabric of sexism. They are seen as betrayers, as traitors who must be punished and eliminated. In the beating and killing of gay men we see clear evidence of this hatred. When we see the fierce homophobia expressed toward gay men, we can begin to understand the ways sexism also affects males through imposing rigid, dehumanizing gender roles on them. The two circumstances in which it is legitimate for men to be openly physically affectionate with one another are in competitive sports and in the crisis of war. For many men, these two experiences are the

18

highlights of their lives, and they think of them again and again with nostalgia. War and sports offer a cover of all-male safety and dominance to keep away the notion of affectionate openness being identified with homosexuality. When gay men break ranks with male roles through bonding and affection outside the arenas of war and sports, they are perceived as not being "real men," that is, as being identified with women, the weaker sex that must be dominated and that over the centuries has been the object of male hatred and abuse. Misogyny gets transferred to gay men with a vengeance and is increased by the fear that their sexual identity and behavior will bring down the entire system of male dominance and compulsory heterosexuality.

If lesbians are established as threats to the status quo, as outcasts who must be punished, homophobia can wield its power over all women through lesbian baiting. Lesbian baiting is an attempt to control women by labeling us as lesbians because our behavior is not acceptable, that is, when we are being independent, going our own way, living whole lives, fighting for our rights, demanding equal pay, saying no to violence, being self-assertive, bonding with and loving the company of women, assuming the right to our bodies, insisting upon our own authority, making changes that include us in society's decision-making; lesbian baiting occurs when women are called lesbians because we resist male dominance and control. And it has little or nothing to do with one's sexual identity.

To be named as lesbian threatens all women, not just lesbians, with great loss. And any woman who steps out of role risks being called a lesbian. To understand how this is a threat to all women, one must understand that any woman can be called a lesbian and there is no real way she can defend herself: there is no way to credential one's sexuality. ("The Children's Hour," a Lillian Hellman play, makes this point when a student asserts two teachers are lesbians and they have no way to disprove it.) She may be married or divorced, have children, dress in the most feminine manner, have sex with men, be celibate—but there are lesbians who do all those things. *Lesbians look like all women and all women look like lesbians.* There is no guaranteed method of identification, and as we all know, sexual identity can be kept hidden. (The same is true for men. There is no way to prove their sexual identity, though many go to extremes to prove heterosexuality.) Also, women are not necessarily born lesbian. Some seem to be, but others become lesbians later in life after having lived heterosexual lives. Lesbian baiting of heterosexual women would not work if there were a definitive way to identify lesbians (or heterosexuals.)

We have yet to understand clearly how sexual identity develops. And this is disturbing to some people, especially those who are determined to discover how lesbian and gay identity is formed so that they will know where to start in eliminating it. (Isn't it odd that there is so little concern about discovering the causes of heterosexuality?) There are many theories: genetic makeup, hormones, socialization, environment, etc. But there is no conclusive evidence that indicates that heterosexuality comes from one process and homosexuality from another.

We do know, however, that sexual identity can be in flux, and we know that sexual identity means more than just the gender of people one is attracted to and has sex with. To be a lesbian has as many ramifications as for a woman to be heterosexual. It is more than sex, more than just the bedroom issue many would like to make it: it is a woman-centered life with all the social interconnections that entails. Some lesbians are in long-term relationships, some in short-term ones, some date, some are celibate, some are married to men, some remain as separate as possible from men, some have children by men, some by alternative insemination, some seem "feminine" by societal standards, some "masculine," some are doctors, lawyers and ministers, some laborers, housewives and writers:

what all share in common is a sexual/affectional identity that focuses on women in its attractions and social relationships.

If lesbians are simply women with a particular sexual identity who look and act like all women, then the major difference in living out a lesbian sexual identity as opposed to a heterosexual identity is that as lesbians we live in a homophobic world that threatens and imposes damaging loss on us for being *who we are*, for choosing to live whole lives. Homophobic people often assert that homosexuals have the choice of not being homosexual; that is, we don't have to act out our sexual identity. In that case, I want to hear heterosexuals talk about their willingness not to act out their sexual identity, including not just sexual activity but heterosexual social interconnections and heterosexual privilege. It is a question of wholeness. It is very difficult for one to be denied the life of a sexual being, whether expressed in sex or in physical affection, and to feel complete, whole. For our loving relationships with humans feed the life of the spirit and enable us to overcome our basic isolation and to be interconnected with humankind.

If, then, any woman can be named a lesbian and be threatened with terrible losses, what is it she fears? Are these fears real? Being vulnerable to a homophobic world can lead to these losses:

• *Employment.* The loss of job leads us right back to the economic connection to sexism. This fear of job loss exists for almost every lesbian except perhaps those who are self-employed or in a business that does not require societal approval. Consider how many businesses or organizations you know that will hire and protect people who are openly gay or lesbian.

• *Family.* Their approval, acceptance, love.

• *Children.* Many lesbians and gay men have children, but very, very few gain custody in court challenges, even if the other parent is a known abuser. Other children may be kept away from us as though gays and lesbians are abusers. There are written and unwritten laws prohibiting lesbians and gays from being foster parents or from adopting children. There is an irrational fear that children in contact with lesbians and gays will become homosexual through influence or that they will be sexually abused. Despite our knowing that 95 percent of those who sexually abuse children are heterosexual men, there are no policies keeping heterosexual men from teaching or working with children, yet in almost every school system in America, visible gay men and lesbians are not hired through either written or unwritten law.

• *Heterosexual privilege and protection.* No institutions, other than those created by lesbians and gays—such as the Metropolitan Community Church, some counseling centers, political organizations such as the National Gay and Lesbian Task Force, the National Coalition of Black Lesbians and Gays, the Lambda Legal Defense and Education Fund, etc.,— affirm homosexuality and offer protection. Affirmation and protection cannot be gained from the criminal justice system, mainline churches, educational institutions, the government.

• *Safety.* There is nowhere to turn for safety from physical and verbal attacks because the norm presently in this country is that it is acceptable to be overtly homophobic. Gay men are beaten on the streets; lesbians are kidnapped and "deprogrammed." The National Gay and Lesbian Task Force, in an extended study, has documented violence against lesbians and gay men and noted the inadequate response of the criminal justice system. One of the major differences between homophobia/heterosexism and racism and sexism is that because of the Civil Rights Movement and the women's movement racism and sexism are expressed more covertly (though with great harm); because there has not been a major, visible lesbian and gay movement, it is permissible to be overtly homophobic in any institution or public forum. Churches spew forth homophobia in the same way they did racism prior to the Civil Rights Movement. Few laws are in place to protect lesbians and gay men, and the criminal justice system is wracked with homophobia.

• *Mental health.* An overtly homophobic world in which there is full permission to treat lesbians and gay men with cruelty makes it difficult for lesbians and gay men to maintain a strong sense of well-being and self-esteem. Many lesbians and gay men are beaten, raped, killed, subjected to aversion therapy, or put in mental institutions. The impact of such hatred and negativity can lead one to depression and, in some cases, to suicide. The toll on the gay and lesbian community is devastating.

• *Community.* There is rejection by those who live in homophobic fear, those who are afraid of association with lesbians and gay men. For many in the gay and lesbian community, there is a loss of public acceptance, a loss of allies, a loss of place and belonging.

• *Credibility.* This fear is large for many people: the fear that they will no longer be respected, listened to, honored, believed. They fear they will be social outcasts.

The list goes on and on. But any one of these essential components of a full life is large enough to make one deeply fear its loss. A black woman once said to me in a workshop, "When I fought for Civil Rights, I always had my family and community to fall back on even when they didn't fully understand or accept what I was doing. I don't know if I could have borne losing them. And you people don't have either with you. It takes my breath away."

What does a woman have to do to get called a lesbian? Almost anything, sometimes nothing at all, but certainly anything that threatens the status quo, anything that steps out of role, anything that asserts the rights of women, anything that doesn't indicate submission and subordination. Assertiveness, standing up for oneself, asking for more pay, better working conditions, training for and accepting a non-traditional (you mean a man's?) job, enjoying the company of women, being financially independent, being in control of one's life, depending first and foremost upon oneself, thinking that one can do whatever needs to be done, but above all, working for the rights and equality of women.

In the backlash to the gains of the women's liberation movement, there has been an increased effort to keep definitions man-centered. Therefore, to work on behalf of women must mean to work against men. To love women must mean that one hates men. A very effective attack has been made against the word *feminist* to make it a derogatory word. In current backlash usage, *feminist* equals *man-hater* which equals *lesbian*. This formula is created in the hope that women will be frightened away from their work on behalf of women. Consequently, we now have women who believe in the rights of women and work for those rights while from fear deny that they are feminists, or refuse to use the word because it is so "abrasive."

So what does one do in an effort to keep from being called a lesbian? She steps back into line, into the role that is demanded of her, tries to behave in such a way that doesn't threaten the status of men, and if she works for women's rights, she begins modifying that work. When women's organizations begin doing significant social change work, they inevitably are lesbian-baited; that is, funders or institutions or community members tell us that they can't work with us because of our "man-hating attitudes" or the presence of lesbians. We are called too strident, told we are making enemies, not doing good.

The battered women's movement has seen this kind of attack: the pressure has been to provide services only, without analysis of the causes of violence against women and strategies for ending it. To provide only services without political analysis

24

or direct action is to be in an approved "helping" role; to analyze the causes of violence against women is to begin the work toward changing an entire system of power and control. It is when we do the latter that we are threatened with the label of man-hater or lesbian. For my politics, if a women's social change organization has not been labeled lesbian or communist, it is probably not doing significant work; it is only "making nice."

Women in many of these organizations, out of fear of all the losses we are threatened with, begin to modify our work to make it more acceptable and less threatening to the male-dominated society which we originally set out to change. The work can no longer be radical (going to the root cause of the problem) but instead must be reforming, working only on the symptoms and not the cause. Real change for women becomes thwarted and stopped. The word *lesbian* is instilled with the power to halt our work and control our lives. And we give it its power with our fear.

In my view, homophobia has been one of the major causes of the failure of the women's liberation movement to make deep and lasting change. (The other major block has been racism.) We were fierce when we set out but when threatened with the loss of heterosexual privilege, we began putting on brakes. Our best-known nationally distributed women's magazine was reluctant to print articles about lesbians, began putting a man on the cover several times a year, and writing articles about women who succeeded in a man's world. We worried about our image, our being all right, our being "real women" despite our work. Instead of talking about the elimination of sexual gender roles, we stepped back and talked about "sex role stereotyping" as the issue. Change around the edges for middleclass white women began to be talked about as successes. We accepted tokenism and integration, forgetting that equality for all women, for all people—and not just equality of white middleclass women with white men—was the goal that we could never put behind us.

But despite backlash and retreats, change is growing from within. The women's liberation movement is beginning to gain strength again because there are women who are talking about liberation for all women. We are examining sexism, racism, homophobia, classism, anti-Semitism, ageism, ableism, and imperialism, and we see everything as connected. This change in point of view represents the third wave of the women's liberation movement, a new direction that does not get mass media coverage and recognition. It has been initiated by women of color and lesbians who were marginalized or rendered invisible by the white heterosexual leaders of earlier efforts. The first wave was the 19th and early 20th century campaign for the vote; the second, beginning in the 1960s, focused on the Equal Rights Amendment and abortion rights. Consisting of predominantly white middleclass women, both failed in recognizing issues of equality and empowerment for all women. The third wave of the movement, multi-racial and multi-issued, seeks the transformation of the world for us all. We know that we won't get there until everyone gets there; that we must move forward in a great strong line, hand in hand, not just a few at a time.

We know that the arguments about homophobia originating from mental health and Biblical/religious attitudes can be settled when we look at the sexism that permeates religious and psychiatric history. The women of the third wave of the women's liberation movement know that *without the existence of sexism, there would be no homophobia.*

Finally, we know that as long as the word lesbian can strike fear in any woman's heart, then work on behalf of women can be stopped; the only successful work against sexism must include work against homophobia.

# The Effect of Homophobia on Women's Liberation

## First, lesbians

THOUGH EVERY WOMAN is hurt by homophobia by its control of her life through fear and by its effect in limiting social change, lesbians suffer the most damage because we are the double victims of sexism/homophobia: from men and from heterosexual women, even feminist or progressive women. A woman who steps outside the rules of patriarchy and threatens its authority expects to be hated and feared by men and those women who find their source of power in men. But she expects to be welcomed by those heterosexual women who are in the struggle to break down the power of male dominance.

Therefore when the second wave of the women's liberation movement began, lesbians thought that at last there was a place where we could be ourselves, a place we could call home among women we could call sisters. Here was the place to work and socialize, to be an open lesbian and to be accepted and understood. If not in the women's movement, then where?

Understandably, lesbians experienced profound despair and rage when we learned that even in this movement to free women there was not a safe place for us, that even here homophobia held women in fear. (Women of color had a similar experience when they thought that here at last was a place that would be free of racism.) Despite the leadership lesbians had had in creating the movement, we were still asked to put the "good of the movement" foremost and to be discreet about our sexual identity, about our lives. Many of us complied because we were accustomed to making our own personal and political needs secondary and because we believed so wholeheartedly in this movement that in the long run was going to free us all. We accepted that our visibility would jeopardize the credibility of the movement.

We had a kind of naive faith that in the end when the liberation of women came, the word *women* would of course include all women—old and young, gentile and Jew, poor and rich, women of color and white women, the temporarily able-bodied and the differently abled, lesbians and non-lesbians—even though some of these people weren't visible in numbers and leadership and agendas now. No one at that time would have to say, like Sojourner Truth, "Ain't I a woman?" I suppose we must have believed in a kind of revelation or conversion politic: that on a certain appointed day we would all stand up together in visibility and solidarity. Our politics were muddled because having had previously too little hope, we now hoped too much.

The best that heterosexual feminists have offered is an acceptance drawn from the politics of tolerance and compassion, not equality. They can accept the idea of lesbians by saying, "The only difference between you and me is who you sleep with. It's just a bedroom issue, just kinky sex in this time of sexual liberation." It is this attitude among feminists, and in the world in general, that causes so much damage to lesbians because by reducing who a lesbian is to a matter of simply sexual activity, they make it easy to take the next step which is to blame lesbians (and gay men) for homophobia.

To say that lesbianism is just a bedroom issue is to deny the wholeness of sexual identity and its social expression, and it denies the presence and effect of homophobia. (Similarly, we deny racism and its devastating effect when white women say to women of color, "I don't see color.") By making it just a bedroom issue (without attendant homophobia) then people feel free to argue that sex should be private and therefore lesbians can and should keep our sex lives private. Why "flaunt it"? If lesbians "flaunt it" (as heterosexuals flaunt their heterosexuality) by talking about who we love, who we spend our time and lives with, how we spend our time that includes others, then we are "inviting" homophobic attacks.

The system that creates the climate for placing the blame on homosexuals is heterosexism. Heterosexism assumes that there is only one way to be, the so-called norm, heterosexual. Heterosexism is backed by institutions, i.e., marriage laws, to ensure its predominance. It is the institutional enforcer of homophobia. Those creating the institutions assume that everyone is of course heterosexual and those who are not are "abnormal" or deviate from the norm. It is acceptable, then, for heterosexuals to be affectionate in public, to talk about their family and social lives, to be open about their social networks and activities, etc., but if homosexuals do, then they say that we are flaunting our deviance. We are endangering ourselves, our families and friends, and the organizations that employ us.

In this way, the victim of homophobia gets blamed for causing the homophobia. (Whites use a similar logic on people of color: "We didn't have racism here until you people came.") Blaming the victim is an essential part of every oppression. At the center of victim blaming is the idea that lesbians simply choose a perverse sexual behavior, an idea sustained by denial of the meaning of sexual identity. To say that to be a lesbian is just a bedroom issue is to say that sexual identity is limited to sexual activity, which doesn't take into account all of the assumptions and behavior that go along with sexual identity. What, for instance, would be the sexual identity of those many heterosexuals and homosexuals who are celibate?

This question was addressed in Phil Donahue's television interview of the editors of *Lesbian Nuns*. As I recall, it went like this. The editors explained how important it was to write the book in order to break the silence about nuns and ex-nuns who are lesbian so that they would not feel isolated and self-blaming. The audience, however, was having difficulty seeing beyond their sense that there was no other purpose to this book than to discredit the Catholic Church. They were not happy. Horrified that nuns still in convent were lesbian, they wanted to know if the editors didn't see this as a sinful breaking of the nun's vows. The editors replied that many of these nuns are celibate.

A woman stood up in the audience and said, "I just don't get it. If you think about stealing and don't steal, you're not a thief. So how can you be a lesbian if you don't have sex?"

EDITORS: "Do you consider yourself heterosexual?"

WOMAN: "Yes, yes, yes."

EDITORS: "Long before you ever had sex with a man, did you know you were heterosexual?"

WOMAN: "Of course."

EDITORS: "That's what we are talking about. Sexual identity."

To say that the issue is only sexual activity leads homophobic people to reason that lesbians simply choose capriciously and perhaps maliciously to have sex with women instead of men. The attitude is that lesbians could stop doing this bad thing if we only wanted to be good: all people supposedly have the ability, though often unused, to be disciplined about sex. But what about all else that sexual identity brings? Physical and affectional intimacy with other people, social interactions, home and family, a hedge against the human condition of aloneness? Who among us wants to give up these things? It seems to me that the pursuit of these things should be the most basic of human rights. If we do not have the right to who we are, to our basic identity, the right to ward off isolation by being connected to other humans, then what do all of our other rights mean?

To see lesbianism as only sexual activity leads people to think first and foremost of sex when they see two lesbians together—or a lesbian and a heterosexual woman. If two lesbians are walking down a street, laughing together, homophobic

30

observers think that of course they are heading toward a place to have sex or are just coming from having had sex. If a lesbian asks a heterosexual woman to dinner, a walk, a movie, then the homophobic response is that it is a movement toward the hope of sex. The homophobic view allows no possibility for friendship, companionship, business associations, the ordinary interactions of a person's life. It fulfills its purpose which is to limit and destroy.

To reduce being a lesbian to sexual activity gives way to the basic mistake that heterosexual women, as victims of sexism, make in thinking about lesbians: they think that if lesbians are sexually attracted to women, then we must think and act sexually like men. Herein is that odd, contradictory and damaging belief: lesbians both hate men and yet we want to be men. Huh???

A stereotype is created: lesbians are masculine, wear short hair and men's clothes, are aggressive, seek non-traditional jobs, and "come on" sexually to heterosexual women. As with all stereotypes, there are a few within the stereotyped group

that fit the description. But like all stereotypes, this one misses the myriad of differences among lesbians, as many differences in looks and behavior as there are among heterosexual women. But stereotypes are the most popular form of keeping in place every oppression, working within the culture to limit and imprison. Hence, many heterosexual women believe that lesbians will pursue them sexually against their will just as men will.

In workshops I've asked women why they fear lesbians and often they'll say, "I'm afraid they'll come on to me sexually." This, from heterosexual women who are approached sexually by men all the time! They can't find the courage to say to a woman, "I'm not interested in sexual involvement with you"? As we talk, they begin to see how deep and irrational their fear is. Inevitably, only one or two at most will have experienced any sexual overtures from a woman but all will attest to having dealt with unwanted sexual advances from men most of their lives.

A few years ago in Arkansas, a bill denying funding to gay and lesbian groups and requiring that all known homosexuals be reported to the proper authorities was submitted to the state legislature. In committee hearing, when the bill's sponsor was asked why he saw the necessity for it, he said that the daughter of a friend of his had been approached by a lesbian in one of her classes at the University of Arkansas. With strong testimony from the lesbian and gay community, the bill failed. If we should hope to keep female students from being sexually approached by *men* in their classes, all of our legislatures and university officials would be kept constantly busy from now until forever. Stereotypes work against all logic.

Because lesbianism is thought to be only sexual activity, there is a belief that one can be "made a lesbian" through sexual activity. Warnings about conversion occur. People fear their children being in the presence of lesbians and gay men. The children of homosexuals are seen at risk of becoming homosexual because of the sexual identity of their parents. Little thought is given to the fact that the vast majority of lesbians and gay men had heterosexual parents and were brought up in a thoroughly heterosexual world. Still, irrationally, people worry about lesbian and gay influence.

This reduction of sexual identity to sexual activity leads feminists to feel justified when they say, "It's OK for you to be a lesbian. Just don't flaunt it. Don't bring it here." Now, just what is *it* that they want us to leave at home? In feminist organizations, lesbians are asked to agree to a trade-off that goes like this: we will let you work here in a liberal atmosphere of tolerance if you in return will make these promises:

• Don't talk about your home life with your partner/lover, or your experiences with your lesbian friends. When you buy a house together, go on trips, suffer losses, celebrate anniversaries, share a car, go grocery shopping together, struggle with your children growing up, have disagreements, separate—don't talk about it here.

• Don't encourage your partner or lesbian friends to pick you up from work or hang around here. We don't want to get the reputation as a lesbian gathering place. Discourage them from calling you here. People will catch on to your relationship.

• Don't give signs that you are a lesbian. Be careful about your dress, the jewelry you wear, the places, people and events you talk about. Assimilate.

• Don't do lesbian organizing, go to marches, or above all, get photographed or televised at a lesbian event. Don't act on behalf of your community.

• Don't try to insert lesbian issues into the women's issues we're working on. Women's rights and lesbian rights are different. Don't keep bringing up homophobia in the organization, confronting people, and causing disorder. Choose between working with us on women's issues or working with homosexuals on lesbian issues.

In other words, the trade-off is that heterosexual feminists will give "tolerance" and the "gift" of recognizing privately that a woman's identity is lesbian, but publicly they want the lesbian identity disappeared, rendered invisible for the greater "good" of women's work. Unlike heterosexual women, lesbians are asked to bring only the asexual, asocial part of ourselves to the feminist workplace. We are asked to behave as though we have no life beyond our work. We are asked to pass. Because of our deep belief in women's liberation and because of our self-blame from internalized homophobia, we often agree to this trade-off. It's difficult to stand strong in the face of the assertion that one's mere presence, one's life, can threaten and possibly destroy an organization, already fragile in a sexist world, that works on behalf of women.

In order to have the privilege of working for women's liberation, lesbians are asked to give up our place in it and are sent politically into exile from the place where our essential women's issues should be addressed and homophobia as a powerful weapon of sexism should be eliminated: in the heart of the women's liberation movement. The sacrifice is great, a tremendous cost to lesbians and all women.

Hence, many lesbians are strong workers and leaders in women's organizations but our political/social identity is not acknowledged, and almost always our work security is tenuous, hanging on a gossamer thread that can be broken by the first hint of lesbian baiting. And what is lesbian baiting? It is a homophobic attack, from either within or outside an organization, that implies or states that the presence of a lesbian or lesbians hurts or discredits the work of the organization. Its purpose is to hurt lesbians, to control all women, and to stop women's social change work.

A lesbian-baiting attack can come from many sources. Let's use a battered women's shelter for an example. It could come from within. Perhaps the volunteer coordinator is a lesbian and in staff meetings she shows strong leadership and advocates a political strategy that some other staff members disagree with, one that perhaps calls for more work or greater problems on their part. Instead of taking on the issue of her ideas and leadership, they begin making behind-the-scenes suggestions about how her being a lesbian hurts the shelter. Quiet discussions are held with a few selected volunteers and they become alarmed at discovering they are working unknowingly with a lesbian. Their homophobia activated, they begin to look for "unusual" behavior. Talk escalates and spreads to the other volunteers. Attention is removed from the work for battered women and focused on the volunteer coordinator who has difficulty defending herself because (1) she is at risk because she is a lesbian in a homophobic world and (2) everything she does now is interpreted in light of her being a lesbian and therefore a sexual threat to both the staff and the women seeking shelter. She is asked to resign or is fired because her work is not effective: the volunteer program has suffered. Work to support battered women and to end violence against women is impaired. And a woman's livelihood has been taken away from her by other women.

Or the lesbian-baiting attack can come from without. Let's stay with the example of the shelter. The attack could come from funders; from institutions that do referrals such as social services, churches, hospitals, police departments; from both community supporters and enemies. The sources are numerous. Economic loss is usually the greatest fear, so suppose in this instance the attack comes from a funder. Making her annual appearance at a United Way meeting, the director of the shelter is told privately by her sympathetic United Way officer that there are deep reservations about the continuation of funding for the shelter because they have heard that it is becoming run by a bunch of lesbians. (As a former NCADV director once said jokingly, lesbians always seem to come in bunches, like bananas.) The shelter director makes assurances that such is not the case, and returns to the shelter, bringing to the staff her fear of impending doom. Attention begins to focus on the work of the lesbian on staff, and it is subjected to fierce scrutiny until something about that work surfaces as inadequate, and she is let go. A flamboyantly heterosexual woman is hired to replace her.

In each of these cases, if the staff person had been a lesbian of color, her jeopardy would have been even greater, for she would have no doubt been under pressure to be an "acceptable" woman of color, and if the only woman of color on staff, she would be expected, overtly or covertly, to represent all women of color. She would be working in the face of racism, sexism and homophobia. If she addressed any of these oppressions, she would no doubt be seen as a troublemaker. For her, a difficult bargain is asked, and with it, tremendous sacrifice of self.

The painful irony of this response to lesbian baiting, for both the lesbian and the organization, is that the lesbian baiting is not stopped—at best there is some temporary appeasement —and women's work for battered women and women's libera- tion has been damaged. And another woman is unemployed. Though in both of these examples a lesbian was on staff, we must remember that the lesbian baiting still would have been effective even if no lesbian had been employed. It is simply the label that creates the fear and control and causes the reduc- tion and modification of our work. Though often unrecognized, the loss to heterosexual women, over time, is equally great, for we all lose our ability to create effective social change.

## And then, heterosexual women

When homophobia wins, all women lose.

Lesbian baiting does not always come in such overt forms as accusations that the organization is a "bunch of lesbians." More often it is couched in terms of concern that the work or goals are too radical, could be construed to be anti-family, anti-male, or man-hating. Or there's an implication that there's something wrong with women who work on behalf of women, that perhaps they are damaged and angry women, or not solid citizens like the "real" women Phyllis Schlafly talks about, those who know their place and are successful because of it.

A "real woman," defined in sexist terms, is submissive, puts the needs of others before her own, is driven by emotions, is indirect, spiritual and innately moral, biologically determined and glad of it, not fully capable, dependent, physically weak, and wisely subordinate to the greater power and wisdom of men. In the same sexist terms it follows that if she is not all these things, then there is something terribly wrong with her; she is to be found at fault for not fulfilling this image. In the book *Annapurna: A Woman's Place*, Arlene Blum, author and leader of the all-women's Annapurna expedition, writes about how she was told before their climb by a male climbing guide that "there are no good women climbers. Women climbers either aren't good climbers, or they aren't real women." (*Sierra Club Books, 1980, Introduction, p. 1.*) By definition, a woman cannot step out of role and still be a "real woman."

It has been the work of the women's liberation movement to change this definition of woman, to set her free from it to be everything she can be, without restriction because of sex. If we accept or feel vulnerable to the sexist definition that to be feminist is to be a man-hater and therefore a lesbian, and want to assert our "normalcy" and acceptability, what happens to our work? What do we feel it is necessary to do to make ourselves acceptable to a sexist world while working to change it?

In order to be safe, we send part of ourselves into exile and assert only the part that has been carefully scrutinized, sanitized as acceptable: a terrible division occurs. The analysis of sexism developed in the early years of the women's liberation movement showed that we had to change attitudes toward the nuclear family, toward sex roles, toward women's educational and economic opportunities, toward compulsory heterosexuality. However, we now have feminists under the threat of homophobia saying to their most trusted inner circle of supporters that although they still believe in the analysis and the work required, they have to live a public life that supports the conventions of sexism.

The conflict between belief and practice leads to alienation, divisiveness, often defensiveness. Women become afraid to work openly for the very things that will set us free, and the fear affects everything in the movement. Hierarchical structures, reflections of the underpinnings of the patriarchy, then continue in women's organizations, along with the management styles that support these structures. Women's organizations often look for directors or leaders who are most heterosexually acceptable in appearance and behavior. Feminists joke about the "dress for success" trend and then adhere to it. Class issues don't get deeply analyzed because to do so would require an equally deep analysis of women's economic role and the economic role of people of color. Despite the ever-increasing visibility of divorced women and men, single parents, widows, lesbians and gay men living in social/family combinations, a piercing critical analysis of the nuclear family and its patriarchal hold does not get made in enough places at enough times. There is not discussion of the fact that the world economy, based on multi-national corporations, has rendered the nuclear family obsolete. Making these analyses in a public forum requires major courage and resistance.

The fear of loss of acceptability is great. But can effective, long-lasting change be made by closet feminists? And to use Audre Lorde's metaphor, can the master's house be dismantled using the master's tools—and I add, by exhibiting only behavior he approves and accepts? Some feminists say, we have to dress this way, talk this way, behave this way, in order to be heard by the men who control the courts, the schools, the institutions that hold power over us.

Such attitudes indicate a belief in benevolence, a belief that people in power can be persuaded to share that power out of decency or goodness. We see enough individual success to be encouraged to go on in this belief: a few women get a small share of power. But the masses of women—women in all our differences of race, class, religion, sexual identity, age, etc.—don't get a share of the power or benefit from it. Therefore, radical women do not believe power, in the broader sense, is ever given freely and benevolently so that all benefit. To gain it, one has to step out of line, grow strong, build a movement of support and identity. One has to gain the consciousness that leads to a different way of acting, the strength and courage to find a different way to live, and when enough find that way and follow it, power shifts. Power resides, of course, only in those we bestow it on. Yielding to those in power by striving to be acceptable to them simply enhances their power and does not bring about lasting social change.

There are ways women lose on the personal level also. In holding back those parts of ourselves that yearn for expression, in limiting who we can be because of fear, we risk living half-lives. In workshops across the country, I ask women what they would have done with their lives if the world had been open to them, without the impediments of sexism. The answers are truly amazing, often profoundly sad. They speak not only of the work they would have trained for, the experiences they would have undertaken, but of the relationships, especially of a non-sexual nature, they would have allowed themselves. They talk of how they held themselves back from people and things that would not be acceptable in a sexist world; how they took roads prescribed for them, rather than those their hearts yearned for; how they suffered such a toll on their mental health and psychic energy; how their true selves now appear

39

only at rare, safe moments and otherwise they live lives that provide safety. They have traded wholeness for heterosexual privilege and survival in a sexist society and they feel in exile from that self that longs for freedom. They want to come home but fear prevents them.

The fear of loss doesn't affect heterosexual women alone. It is the same fear, intensified, that also affects lesbians and causes us to choose various degrees of invisibility. We achieve invisibility by acting out heterosexuality. The enforcement of compulsory heterosexuality is so severe that it takes a major act of resistance to stand against it. It is for that reason that much of our resistance, even among lesbians who by our very lives challenge men's access to women, is underground.

The essay that has most influenced my thought on this subject is Adrienne Rich's brilliant *Compulsory Heterosexuality and Lesbian Existence*, in which she demonstrates that compulsory heterosexuality has been so fierce and inflicted so many great losses that we don't know at this point if women are heterosexual or "choose" heterosexuality in order to survive. (Antelope Publications, 1982, first published in *Signs*, 1980)

In this essay, Rich begins with Kathleen Gough's list of the characteristics of male power in archaic and contemporary society first developed in the essay, "The Origin of the Family," and expounds on these characteristics as being enforcers of compulsory heterosexuality. These characteristics are "men's ability to deny women sexuality or to force it upon them; to command or exploit their labor to control their produce; to control or rob them of their children; to confine them physically and prevent their movement; to use them as objects in male transactions; to cramp their creativeness; or to withhold from them large areas of the society's knowledge and cultural attainments." For each of these characteristics, Rich examines the ways male power is enforced. Her conclusion is that "we are confronting not a simple maintenance of inequality and property possession, but a pervasive cluster of forces, ranging from physical brutality to control of consciousness, which suggests that an enormous potential counterforce is having to be restrained." (*Ibid, pp. 10-12*)

The suggestion is that women might not "choose" heterosexuality if we were not coerced in such damaging ways; many instead might bond with women and the effect would be a change in the locus of power because there would no longer be the "means of assuring male right of physical, economical, and emotional access." (*Ibid, p. 19*)

One important aspect of Rich's approach in this discussion is that she does not argue the necessity for all women to find our deepest sexual and emotional attachments to women or to men but that the "compulsory" be taken out of heterosexuality, that it not be held up as the norm, and in making this change, to take the weight of power out of the hands of men.

To make this change, women will have to resist compulsory heterosexuality and risk its coercive and damaging force. Already there is a tradition of resisting male domination, women who stepped out of line: lesbians, witches, marriage resisters of all kinds— "old maids," spinsters, female religious communities—woman-identified feminists, women who choose not to bear children, widows who choose bonding with women instead of marrying again. (*Ibid, p. 7*)

A major way to resist compulsory heterosexuality and male domination is to eliminate homophobia and heterosexism. Women have to analyze homophobia's power over our lives as it works to coerce heterosexuality. Consciousness must be forged about the ways one's heterosexuality is asserted and the ways one assumes others are heterosexual. We must take a look at the limits it places on our lives. And especially we must examine the fear we have about losing its privileges, the sacrifices we make to keep those privileges, and the ways we are threatened by those who choose to resist.

41

There are some small ways a heterosexual woman might test her progress in eliminating homophobia in her life. When asked if she is a lesbian, she might say, "I'm not a lesbian but I support women's sexual choices," thus distancing and protecting herself. If instead, without asserting her sexual identity, she refuses to allow an issue and judgment to be made about sexual identity, she maintains the clear vision that homophobia is the problem and that the questioner, the accuser, is the source of the problem. Then, if nothing else works to deflect interest in sexual identity, she could choose a version of the Denmark solution: "All women are lesbians and therefore I'm a lesbian too." Heterosexual women must find the freedom to bond openly with both non-lesbians and lesbians without public assertion of their heterosexuality to assure (even if tentatively) their safety. We have to remove the negative power from the word *lesbian* so that it no longer has any force as a weapon against us.

Another test is to think of her children or the young ones in her life. When a child says, "Mother (or aunt or friend or sister), I have fallen in love with a woman," if the first response is "I'm so happy you are in love" and the second is "How can I be supportive?" then it's clear that the concern is her happiness, not the gender she has chosen to love. The other legitimate concern is how to support her in a homophobic world.

And finally, there's always this exercise for heterosexually identified women: write a letter to someone you love intensely whose loss you would find devastating or someone who has power in your life, telling them you are a lesbian. Explore the fears this letter writing calls up and analyze their source and their power over you.

It is only when we can face our fears and resist homophobic/heterosexist assumptions and attacks that we can begin to end male power and control over our lives. At issue here is not whether women can be married or have children or wear makeup and heels; at issue is whether women make choices against our best interests of independence and freedom in order to gain conditional approval and protection at a high cost. At issue here is not whether men take on parenting or household chores and thereby ease the burden of women; instead the issue is the institutional and individual entrenchment of male power and the coercive nature of that power. At issue here is not that all women should be lesbians in order to be free, but that we understand that women's struggles for independence and freedom and self-empowerment are identified with lesbians as a way to frighten women away from them, and that all of us as women need to look at our response to lesbian baiting and what blocks our empowerment. At issue is not just our sexual identity but our freedom.

# Strategies for Eliminating Homophobia

AS FREUD supposedly asked in frustration about women, "What *do* women want?" some heterosexual feminists might ask about lesbians, "What do they want, anyway? Haven't we given them enough?" It can be argued that many feminist organizations have lesbians in places of leadership, but we have to remember that most of us have had to pay a damaging price in the trade-offs we have made in order to be an accepted part of the organization. And we have to remember how many "unacceptable" lesbians—those who don't reflect heterosexuality—have not been included in the front and visible lines of the women's liberation movement.

So what do lesbians want? We want the elimination of homophobia. We are seeking equality. Equality is more than tolerance, compassion, understanding, acceptance, benevolence, for these still come from a place of implied superiority: favors granted to those less fortunate. These attitudes suggest that there is still something wrong, something not quite right that must be overlooked or seen beyond. The elimination of homophobia requires that homosexual identity be viewed as viable and legitimate and as normal as heterosexual identity. It does not require tolerance; it requires an equal footing. Given the elimination of homophobia, sexual identity—whether homosexual, bi-sexual, or heterosexual—will not be seen as good or bad but simply as what is.

With homophobia eliminated, we will be able to remove our concern about the gender of the person one loves and apply it instead to those areas where people abuse one another with their sexual practices: incest, rape, objectification of sexual partners, pornography, and all forms of coercive sex, including marital rape. Our concern in relationships can then center on crucial power, dominance, and control issues, not the gender of the relationship partners. There is precious little enough love, affection, and tenderness in the world; it would be a great step forward for humankind if we granted people their right to love.

How then do we begin to eliminate homophobia in our personal lives and in our women's organizations? We must begin the way we begin all the things we do successfully: by setting achievable goals and taking small steps that eventually lead to larger steps. The overall goal is to strip homophobia of its power and thereby eliminate it. To stop that power, we must stop contributing to it.

A very small but powerful and effective first step we can take is to say the word *lesbian*. We must say it in positive ways in our everyday conversations as we affirm different sexual identities, and we must say the word *lesbian* when we talk about our work with women. It is not enough to say that our women's organization is for all women because women from groups that have never been considered the norm are still rendered invisible under the term *all women*. For years people, including feminists, have talked about *women* and meant *white women* in their assumptions and in their descriptions: women of color were rendered both invisible and left out. The same has been true of old women, differently abled women, women who aren't Christian, poor women, and certainly lesbians. We must bring truth and integrity to our words: when we say all women, we must mean *all* women.

If we are to succeed in the liberation of women, it will have to be through all of us working together for goals that include us all. Therefore, a primary strategy has to be inclusiveness, not only in the ranks but in the decision-making and sharing of power. Because women are affected by other oppressions in addition to sexism, we must understand the connections

46

among those oppressions, work to eliminate them, and acknowledge those groups of women who have been systematically excluded from the privileges shared by those considered the "norm." Until those oppressions are eliminated, we cannot use the expression "all women" and expect women and the world at large to know that every kind of woman is included. Until true inclusion happens, we must name all the women we mean until everyone everywhere understands we are engaged in a movement to free all women.

Moreover, we must demonstrate that we are engaged in work that directly affects different groups of women. What many organizations have done in the past is an ineffective form of "outreach." Women's organizations that are primarily white in their top staff positions and boards of directors begin reaching out to communities of color, asking women to join them in ways that don't include participation in vital decision-making or ownership—and then they are disappointed and angry that women of color do not join. We see battered women's shelters reaching out to women of color or battered lesbians before they have done crucial work on racism and homophobia, thus subjecting women of color and lesbians to the additional violence of racism and homophobia in their organizations. Hence, when we say "all women," we must specify all those we wish to include, and our programs and services must reflect a full commitment to diversity. When we are truly diverse in the ownership of our programs, women will know they are included and will join in the work that touches all of us. Our reputation and our track record will be our "outreach."

At present the word *lesbian* holds tremendous power, is highly charged, and instills fear in heterosexual women and in lesbians who have chosen invisibility. Just as visible lesbians are not so vulnerable to being named lesbian, so are women's organizations less vulnerable to lesbian baiting when they are open and strong about the inclusion of lesbians in their work with all women. The word's power begins to be diminished in the face of those who refuse to concede its negative power.

As long as women's organizations are afraid to use the word *lesbian* in public speeches, in written materials, in grants, then those organizations are not safe places for lesbians to work or to seek services. If the word still holds such power that it cannot be used, then that is clear evidence that the organization is not willing or able to support and defend lesbians in its ranks. If it will not take the initial risk of saying the word, then what would make us believe there would be any risk-taking in the face of threats or controversy? This fear makes fertile ground for lesbian baiting.

Battered women's programs that want to work with battered lesbians must understand that it is not safe for a battered lesbian or lesbian staff to participate if the program does not talk about lesbians in its brochures, public speeches, grant proposals. Needless to say, battered lesbians can't learn about the program unless battered lesbians are talked about in the program's general public information—lesbians are everywhere the general population is. Until programs have worked on homophobia and are prepared to face lesbian baiting, they should not offer services to lesbians within the shelter.

We must find ways to confront lesbian-baiting. One of the most effective is to keep the problem clearly focused on the homophobic person, not on the woman or organization. The problem is with the person who hates, who is prejudiced, not with the victim. If someone says, "I understand your organization has turned into just a bunch of lesbians," then we begin asking questions such as, "What is the problem you have with different sexual identities?" "What is it about you that is threatened by lesbians?" "Why do you think what lesbians are doing is harmful?" "What experiences led you to develop this prejudice?" If we are clear about the right people have to their sexual identity, then it is not necessary for us to be defensive. Nor do we have to be antagonistic or violent. Instead, we can assist people in understanding and accepting people's right to sexual identity or at least understanding that their homophobia, with its restrictions on human relationships, is the problem.

Another small step is to drop assumptions of heterosexual identity on the part of others. Upon first conversations with an adult woman, most people ask, are you married, do you have children? This immediate assumption leaves those who are not married or who have no children to feel there is something wrong with them and their lives and choices or circumstances. The questions also reinforce the belief that woman's most important role is as a married mother. When gatherings and parties are held in women's organizations, many women still assume heterosexuality and ask women to invite husbands or dates instead of simply asking that women invite those we care for, whether they are friends, sexual partners, or relatives.

Along with dropping these assumptions, we need to look at what it is about ourselves that we put forward in order to prove we are acceptable, at the ways we assert that we are heterosexually identified. Is the first thing asserted that one is married or attached to men in some way? How weary I am of feminists who feel they have to be excessively reassuring that they like men. What has always amused and amazed me is that the very worst things I have ever heard said about men have been by married (frequently non-feminist) women, not lesbians, especially longtime lesbians. Still, women feel the necessity to distance themselves from lesbians by asserting how much they *like* men. Liking men is not the issue. Freedom from dominance and control is the issue, and that's why married women talk so angrily and disparagingly about the men who dominate them in traditional marriages that don't have societal support for women's equality.

49

Instead of distancing oneself from lesbians, one must confront homophobia by being openly supportive of lesbian identity, both in personal and public life and in feminist work. Support means not requiring invisibility or disappearances. Support means being as engaged in the lives of lesbians as in the lives of heterosexual women, sharing sorrow and happiness, participating in the rites of couple bonding, in the rites of passage, and by honoring those things as being important, as being valid events in an individual's life. A lesbian's separation from her partner is no less serious than a heterosexual's divorce. A lesbian falling in love is an occasion for as much joy as a heterosexual falling in love. And we must honor and affirm the choice of both lesbians and heterosexuals to live alone.

Another way to support lesbian identity is to appreciate lesbian culture and to participate in it. On the personal level, this means reading some of the many books and periodicals written by lesbians, listening to lesbian music and attending concerts and music festivals, seeing and discussing lesbian films and videos. It is this participation that will begin the work to eliminate stereotyping, for it is within the lesbian culture that we see the incredible diversity of lesbian lives. To do more than just raise personal consciousness and ensure personal growth, one has to talk about this appreciation and participation in a public way, for it is the sharing of one's growth and consciousness that brings about the social change necessary to eliminate homophobia.

In our women's organizations, we must make lesbian culture visible—in the books and periodicals and records and paintings we purchase and share with our constituencies in an open and proud way. While presenting current lesbian culture, we must also do work to reclaim the past. Because homophobia has been so fierce, lesbian history and work in the movement has been destroyed, has been rendered invisible. Writings about women's history and women's feminist work often read as though contributions were made primarily by white heterosexual women. As we have begun reclaiming women's history from its disappearance among men's history, we now must work harder to reclaim the history of lesbians and women of color.

Along with working on support for lesbian visibility, we must integrate an analysis of homophobia, heterosexism and compulsory heterosexuality in our work against sexism and develop strategies to eliminate these related oppressions. We must make a public commitment to work for a world where sexual identity and sexual roles are not coerced and restricted, a world where no one is granted the socially condoned power to dominate and control others because of sexual gender and identity.

To do this work of eliminating homophobia is no easy task, for there are great risks involved. It is currently acceptable to be overtly homophobic: to make jokes about gays and lesbians, to say in state legislatures that AIDS is only important when it hits the heterosexual population, to pass and uphold sodomy laws, to forbid lesbians and gays from providing foster care to children, to overlook school children calling each other "faggot," to issue court decisions that withhold custody from lesbian mothers, to hold police raids on gay bars and physically and emotionally harass customers, to hear about the beating and killing of gay men and to dismiss it as deserved.

However, overt oppressions exist only when there is covert expression of these oppressions and support for them. As Elie Wiesel said in a television interview after receiving the Nobel Peace Prize, in Nazi Germany when the concentration camps were being developed, the public silence was deafening. Our own silence is a major contributor to overt homophobia—when we laugh at homophobic jokes or don't speak out, when we yield to lesbian baiting, when we require heterosexual behavior from lesbians and gay men, when we stereotype and call the exceptions the good lesbians or gay men, as in "You would never guess she/he was gay."

We must take a very hard look at our complicity with oppressions, all of them. We must see that to give no voice, to take no action to end them is to support their existence. Our options are two: to be racist, or anti-Semitic, or homophobic (or whatever the oppression may be), or to work actively against these attitudes. There is no middle ground. With an oppression such as homophobia where there is so much permission to sustain overt hatred and injustice, one must have the courage to take the risks that may end in loss of privilege. We must keep clearly in mind, however, that privilege earned from oppression is always conditional and is gained at the cost of freedom.

# The Common Elements
# of Oppressions

I T IS VIRTUALLY impossible to view one oppression, such as sexism or homophobia, in isolation because they are all connected: sexism, racism, homophobia, classism, ableism, anti-Semitism, ageism. They are linked by a common origin—economic power and control—and by common methods of limiting, controlling and destroying lives. There is no hierarchy of oppressions. Each is terrible and destructive. To eliminate one oppression successfully, a movement has to include work to eliminate them all or else success will always be limited and incomplete.

To understand the connection among the oppressions, we must examine their common elements. The first is a *defined norm*, a standard of rightness and often righteousness wherein all others are judged in relation to it. This norm must be backed up with institutional power, economic power, and both institutional and individual violence. It is the combination of these three elements that makes complete power and control possible. In the United States, that norm is male, white, heterosexual, Christian, temporarily able-bodied, youthful, and has access to wealth and resources. It is important to remember that an established norm does not necessarily represent a majority in terms of numbers; it represents those who have ability to exert power and control over others.

It is also important to remember that this group has to have *institutional* power. For instance, I often hear people say that they know people of color in this country who are racist. This is confusing racism with bigotry or prejudice or hatred. People of color simply do not have institutional power to back up their hatred or bigotry or prejudice and therefore cannot be deemed racist. In the same way, women do not have the power to institutionalize their prejudices against men, so there is no such thing as "reverse sexism." How do we know this? We simply have to take a look at the representation of women and people of color in our institutions. Take, for example, the U.S. Congress. What percentage of its members are people of color or women? Or look at the criminal justice system which carries out the laws the white males who predominate in Congress create: how many in that system are people of color? And then when we look at the percentage of each race that is incarcerated, that is affected by these laws, we see that a disproportionate number are people of color. We see the same lack of representation in financial institutions, in the leadership of churches and synagogues, in the military.

In our schools, the primary literature and history taught are about the exploits of white men, shown through the white man's eyes. Black history, for instance, is still relegated to one month, whereas "American history" is taught all year round. Another major institution, the media, remains controlled and dominated by white men and their images of themselves.

In order for these institutions to be controlled by a single group of people, there must be *economic power.* Earlier I discussed the necessity to maintain racism and sexism so that people of color and women will continue to provide a large pool of unpaid or low-paid labor. Once economic control is in the hands of the few, all others can be controlled through limiting access to resources, limiting mobility, limiting employment options. People are pitted against one another through perpetuation of the *myth of scarcity* which suggests that our resources are limited and blames the poor for using up too much of what little there is to go around. It is this myth that is called forth, for instance, when those in power talk about immigration through our southern borders (immigrants who also happen to be people of color). The warning is clear: if you let these people in, they will take your jobs, ruin your schools which are already in economic struggle, destroy the few neighborhoods that are good for people to live in. People are pitted against one another along race and class lines. Meanwhile, those who have economic power continue to make obscenely excessive profits, often by taking their companies out of the country into economically depressed countries occupied by people of color where work can be bought for miniscule wages and profits are enormous. It is not the poor or workingclass population that is consuming and/or destroying the world's resources; it is those who make enormous profits from the exploitation of those resources, the top 10 percent of the population.

That economic power ensures control of institutions. Let's go back to the example of the Congress. How much does it cost to run a campaign to be elected to the House or Senate? One does not find poor people there, for in order to spend the hundreds of thousands of dollars that campaigns cost, one has to be either personally rich or well connected to those who are rich. And the latter means being in the debt, one way or another, of the rich. Hence, when a congressperson speaks or votes, who does he (occasionally she) speak for? Those without access to wealth and resources or those who pay the campaign bills? Or look at the criminal justice system. It is not by chance that crimes against property are dealt with more seriously than crimes against persons. Or that police response to calls from well-to-do neighborhoods is more efficient than to poor neighborhoods. Schools in poor neigborhoods in most instances lack good facilities and resources; and a media that is controlled by advertising does not present an impartial, truthseeking vision of the world. Both schools and the media present what is in the best interest of the prevailing norm.

The maintenance of societal and individual power and control requires the use of *violence and the threat of violence.*

Institutional violence is sanctioned through the criminal justice system and the threat of the military—for quelling individual or group uprisings. One of the places we can most readily see the interplay of institutional and individual violence is in the white man's dealings with the native American population. Since the white man first "discovered" this country, which was occupied by large societies of Indians who maintained their own culture, religion, politics, education, economy and justice, the prevailing norm has been to lay claim to land and resources for those who have the power to establish control by might and thus ensure their superior economic position. This "might" brings with it a sense of superiority and often of divine right. The native Americans were driven from their land and eventually placed (some would say incarcerated) on reservations. By defending their lands and their lives, they became the "enemy." Consequently, we now have a popular culture whose teaching of history represents the native American as a cruel savage and through hundreds of films shows the white man as civilized and good in pursuing his destiny and the native American as bad in protecting his life and culture. Institutional racism is so complete that now great numbers of native Americans, having lost their land and having had their culture assaulted, live in poverty and in isolation from the benefits of mainstream culture. And on the personal level, racism is so overt that television stations still run cowboy-and-Indian movies, and parents buy their children cowboy-and-Indian outfits so that they can act out genocide in their play.

For gay men and lesbians this interplay of institutional and personal violence comes through both written and unwritten laws. In the 25 states that still have sodomy laws, there is an increase in tolerance for violence against lesbians and gay men, whether it is police harassment or the lack of police protection when gay and lesbian people are assaulted. The fact that courts in many states deny custody to gay and lesbian parents, that schools, either through written or unwritten policy, do not hire openly gay and lesbian teachers creates a climate in which it is permissible to act out physical violence toward lesbian and gay people.

And as I discussed in an earlier chapter, for all groups it is not just the physical violence that controls us but the ever constant *threat of violence*. For women, it is not just the rape or battering or the threat of these abuses but also that one's life is limited by the knowledge that one quite likely will not be honored in court. The violence is constantly nurtured by institutions that do not respect those different from the norm. Thus, the threat of violence exists at every level.

There are other ways the defined norm manages to maintain its power and control other than through institutional power, economic power and violence. One way the defined norm is kept an essentially closed group is by a particular system known as *lack of prior claim*. At its simplest, this means that if you weren't there when the original document (the Constitution, for instance) was written or when the organization was first created, then you have no right to inclusion. Since those who wrote the Constitution were white male property owners who did not believe in the complete humanity of either women or blacks, then these two groups have had to battle for inclusion. If women and people of color were not in business (because of the social and cultural restrictions on them) when the first male business organizations were formed, then they now have to fight for inclusion. The curious thing about lack of prior claim is that it is simply the circumstances of the moment that put the orginal people there in every case, yet when those who were initially excluded begin asking for or demanding inclusion, they are seen as disruptive people, as trouble-makers, as no doubt anti-American. We still recall the verbal and physical violence against women who participated in the Suffrage Movement and the black men and women who formed the Civil

Rights Movement. For simply asking for one's due, one was vilified and abused. This is an effective technique, making those struggling for their rights the ones in the wrong. Popular movements are invalidated and minimized, their participants cast as enemies of the people, and social change is obstructed by those holding power who cast themselves as defenders of tradition and order.

Those who seek their rights, who seek inclusion, who seek to control their own lives instead of having their lives controlled are the people who fall outside the norm. They are defined in relation to the norm and are found lacking. They are *the Other.* If they are not part of the norm, they are seen as abnormal, deviant, inferior, marginalized, not "right," even if they as a group (such as women) are a majority of the population. They are not considered fully human. By those identified as the Norm, the Other is unknown, difficult to comprehend, whereas the Other always knows and understands those who hold power; one has to in order to survive. As in the television series "Upstairs, Downstairs," the servants always knew the inner workings of the ruling families' lives while the upstairs residents who had economic control knew little of the downstairs workers' lives. In slavery, the slave had to know the complexity, the inner workings of the slaveowners' lives in order to protect him/herself from them.

The Other's existence, everyday life, achievements are kept unknown through *invisibility.* When we do not see the differently abled, the aged, gay men and lesbians, people of color on television, in movies, in educational books, etc., there is reinforcement of the idea that the Norm is the majority and others either do not exist or do not count. Or when there is false information, *distortion* of events, through selective presentation or the re-writing of history, we see only the negative aspects or failures of a particular group. For instance, it has been a major task of the Civil Rights Movement and the women's movement to write blacks and women back into history and to correct the distorted versions of their history that have been presented over centuries.

This distortion and lack of knowledge of the Other expresses itself in *stereotyping*, that subtle and effective way of limiting lives. It is through stereotyping that people are denied their individual characteristics and behavior and are dehumanized. The dehumanizing process is necessary to feed the oppressor's sense of being justified and to alleviate the feeling of guilt. If one stereotypes all gay men as child molestors and gives them the daily humiliations of perjorative names, such as "faggot," or "cocksucker," then a school administration can feel justified, even righteous, in not hiring them, and young heterosexual males can feel self-righteous when physically attacking them on the streets. In stereotyping, the actions of a few dictate the classification of the entire group while the norm is rarely stereotyped. Because of the belief that groups outside the norm think and behave in unified stereotypical ways, people who hold power will often ask a person of color, "What do your people think about this idea (or thing)?" When do we ever ask a white man, "What do the white men in this country (or organization) think about this?" They are expected to have and to express individual judgments and opinions.

Stereotyping contributes to another common element of oppressions: *blaming the victim* for the oppression. In order for oppression to be thoroughly successful, it is necessary to involve the victim in it. The victim lives in an environment of negative images (stereotypes) and messages, backed up by violence, victim-hating and blaming, all of which leads to low self-esteem and self-blame in the victim. The oppression thus becomes internalized. The goal of this environment is to lead the victim to be complicit with her/his victimization: to think that it is deserved and should not be resisted.

Some of the best work feminists have done is to change

attitudes from blaming the victim to blaming the abuser, a very slow change that is still incomplete. It is no longer automatically the norm to blame victims of battering, rape and incest for having somehow been responsible for the harm done them; instead, people are more inclined to stop supporting male dominance by protecting the abuser. However, we have yet to examine thoroughly the blame we put on victims of racism, homophobia and anti-Semitism. People are condemned for being who they are, for their essence as humans. When we are clear of these oppressions, we will understand that the issue is not one's racial, ethnic, religious or sexual identity—one should have the inalienable right to be who one is—but the problem is racism, sexism, anti-Semitism, and homophobia and the power they support and protect.

Blaming the victims for their oppression diverts attention from the true abuser or the cause of the victimization. For example, a commonly held belief is that people are poor because they are unwilling to work. The belief is supported by the stereotypes that poor people are lazy, abuse welfare, etc. What goes unnoted is the necessity for poverty in an economic system in which wealth is held and controlled by the few. If the poor are in poverty because they deserve it, then the rich need not feel any guilt or compunction about their concentrated wealth. In fact, they can feel deserving and superior.

Blaming the victim leads to the victim feeling complicit with the oppression, of deserving it. As one takes in the negative messages and stereotypes, there is a weakening of self-esteem, self pride and group pride. When the victim of the oppression is led to believe the negative views of the oppressor, this phenomenon is called *internalized oppression*. It takes the form of self-hatred which can express itself in depression, despair, and self-abuse. It is no surprise, therefore, that the incidence of suicide is high among gay men and lesbians, for they live in a world in which messages of hatred and disgust are unrelenting. Nor is it surprising that the differently abled come to think there is no hope for their independence or for them to receive basic human services, for they are taught that the problem is with them, not society. Any difference from the norm is seen as a deficiency, as bad.

Sometimes the internalized oppression is acted out as *horizontal hostility*. If one has learned self-hatred because of one's membership in a "minority" group, then that disrespect and hatred can easily be extended to the entire group so that one does not see hope or promise for the whole. It is safer to express hostility toward other oppressed peoples than toward the oppressor. Hence, we see people destroying their own neighborhoods, displaying violence and crime toward their own people, or in groups showing distrust of their own kind while respecting the power of those who make up the norm. Sometimes the internalized oppression leads people to be reluctant to associate with others in their group. Instead, their identity is with those in power. Hence, a major part of every social change movement has been an effort to increase the pride and self-esteem of the oppressed group, to bond people together for the common good.

A major component of every oppression is *isolation*. Victims of oppressions are either isolated as individuals or as a "minority" group. Take, for example, those who experience rape or incest or battering. Prior to the women's movement and the speak-outs that broke the silence on these issues, women who had experienced abuse were isolated from one another, thought they were alone in experiencing it, and thought, as society dictated, that they were to blame for the abuse. It was through women coming together in the anti-violence movement that we learned that indeed there was something larger going on, that violence was happening to millions of women; out of that coming together grew an analysis of male power and control that led to a movement to end violence against women.

Another example: before the Civil Rights Movement, there were black citizens in the South who were isolated because of their lack of access to resources, in this case, to education and literacy. Because they could not read, they could not pass the tests that allowed them to vote. The Citizenship Schools that began on St. Johns Island, South Carolina, taught blacks to read the Constitution so that they could pass the test; in reading the Constitution, they learned that they too had rights. These schools spread across the South; people came together out of their isolation, and a Civil Rights Movement was born.

In order to break down the power and control exercised by the few, it is clear that people of all oppressed groups must come together to form a movement that speaks for everyone's rights. People will gain their human rights, justice,and inclusion through group effort, not through isolated individual work. However, those who hold power oppose group organizing efforts and use many strategies to destroy such efforts: invalidation, miminization, intimidation, infiltration, etc.

Two of the more subtle ways that society blocks solidarity within groups from ever occurring are the tactics of *assimilation and tokenism.* There are extraordinary pressures for members of any "minority" group to assimilate, to drop one's own culture and differences and become a mirror of the dominant culture. This process requires turning one's back on one's past and on one's people. Assimilation supports the myth of the melting pot in which all immigrants were poured in, mixed a bit, and then emerged as part of the dominant culture: white, heterosexual, and Christian.

Assimilation is a first requirement of those who are chosen as tokens in the workplace of the dominant culture. "She's a Jew but she doesn't act like a Jew." "He's black but he's just like us." Tokenism is the method of limited access that gives false hope to those left behind and blames them for "not making it." "If these two or three black women or disabled people

62

can make it, then what is wrong with you that you can't?" Tokenism is a form of co-optation. It takes the brightest and best of the most assimilated, rewards them with position and money (though rarely genuine leadership and power), and then uses them as a model of what is necessary to succeed, even though there are often no more openings for others who may follow their model.

The tokenized person receives pressure from both sides. From those in power there is the pressure to be separate from one's group (race, for instance) while also acting as a representative of the entire group. "We tried hiring a person of color but it just didn't work out." (Therefore people of color can't succeed here.) The tokenized person is expected to become a team player which means that identifying racist activity within the organization or working on behalf of one's community is seen as disloyalty. The pressure from one's community, on the other hand, is to fight for that community's concerns, in other words, to help from the inside. Of course, it is virtually impossible to work from the inside because the tokenized person is isolated and lacks support. It is a "no win" situation, filled with frustration and alienation.

At the heart of this strategy, which gets played out at every level of society, is an individualized approach to success. The example of Horatio Alger and the notion of "pulling oneself up by the bootstraps" still lives. Daily news reports do not show successful organizing efforts; in fact, the media minimize even undeniably successful ones as was the case with the reporting of the 1988 Gay and Lesbian March on Washington. The media reported the march to have 200,000 in attendance when it was announced by Jesse Jackson from the stage that police and march organizers were reporting over 500,000 there. Instead of reporting group efforts, the media concentrates on "human interest" stories, following the lead of people such as Ronald Reagan who give accounts of individuals who beat the odds and succeed. They become "models" for others in their circumstances to follow. But what good are models when closed systems do not permit general success?

Group organizing, even among progressive people, often gets replaced by an emphasis on *individual solutions*. Hence, instead of seeking ways to develop an economic system that emphasizes cooperation and shared wealth, people encourage entrepreneurship and small business enterprises. Union organizing is under seige in an effort to keep labor costs low and profits high. In the women's movement, more women choose individual therapy rather than starting or joining consciousness raising groups. In the area of health, communities do major organizing, for example, to raise enormous funds to provide a liver transplant for an individual child but do not work together to change the medical system so that all who need them can get organ transplants. The emphasis upon individual solutions is counter to movement making, to broad social change. The emphasis upon individual achievement feeds right into blaming those who don't succeed for their failure. It separates people rather than bringing them together to make change.

We must find ways to build coalition, to make broad social change for all of us. There are many more people who are considered the Other (though called, ironically, the minority) than those who are defined as the Norm. We must become allies in a movement that works against power and control by the few and for shared power and resources for the many. To do this work, we will have to build a program that provides an analysis of the oppressions, their connections, and together we must seek ways to change those systems that limit our lives.

# Women in Exile:
# The Lesbian Experience

## Internalized Homophobia:
## The Damage of a Homophobic World

WHEN GIVING workshops on internalized homophobia, I often ask all the lesbians who grew up in that city or that area to hold up their hands. Almost always the number is fewer than 25 percent, sometimes fewer than 10 percent. When I ask the others why they left their childhood homes and families, the majority say they had to leave in order to find a place where they could live with some freedom as lesbians. They were seeking wholeness. They speak of missing close connections with family loved ones, of seeking a sense of community, of creating families. Fearing loss of their families and communities if they stayed among them identified as lesbians, they left so that they could live a little more visibly in a place where they were not known. They are in exile, seeking freedom.

Many of the lesbians I meet have been deeply wounded by the ravages of homophobia. Some have told their families they were lesbian and were rejected; others were accepted but only conditionally so. Some have lost jobs, custody of children, acceptance in the church of their choice, friends; others have been incarcerated in prisons or mental institutions. Some have left their homes and families to live far away, only to learn that there is little acceptance of their sexual identity anywhere. Feeling so much alienation from the heterosexual world, many have put all their hopes and needs into their love relationships or their lesbian communities and have felt anger and despair when both showed human failings. Some have lived defiantly in the face of homophobia; others have chosen complete invisibility. All have been touched by homophobia, even those who with great courage have lived their lives openly as lesbians and maintained good self-esteem and achieved success in their work and home lives.

What I have found in these workshops is that lesbians are survivors. Despite the harsh damaging effects of homophobia, we have created a magnificent lesbian culture of books and music and crafts and film and paintings and newspapers and periodicals. We have created social communities in cities, lesbian land communities in rural areas, and retirement communities for older lesbians. With little support except from other lesbians, we have created lesbian counseling centers, support groups for chemically dependent lesbians, coffee houses, lesbian retreats and art festivals and music festivals, healing centers, outdoors clubs, support groups for lesbian survivors of battering, rape and incest, rituals for our passages and our spirituality, support groups for lesbian mothers, lesbians of color, differently abled lesbians, Jewish lesbians. The list goes on and on.

Individually, we are also miracles of survival. In the face of society's homophobia, we constantly assess our safety and determine how visible we can be at any moment. We ask ourselves: How much of my self can I put forward in this moment? Is this friend trustworthy? Will this stranger physically attack me? What will be the response if these people know? Homophobia causes us to engage in a juggling act of our identity in order to survive. And yet we do and most of us manage to maintain sanity and health.

We live in a world in which it is not safe to be a lesbian, in which we risk terrible losses, yet we know it is only through our visibility that we will gain any freedom, either individually or collectively. Sometimes our lives feel like living on a double-edged sword: if we choose visibility, we may lose our families, children, friends, jobs, lives; but if we choose invisibility, we still are at risk of losing those things while living under the extra burden of living a double life, and our invisibility makes us unable to know who other lesbians are, thereby making it almost impossible to create a lesbian movement. Invisibility makes us live in isolation and feeds the power of homophobia over our lives. Each time we yield to it, we attest to its power. We know that power will be broken only when large groups of people say no to it: hence, when lesbians and gay men find the courage to risk visibility, the victory is both for their individual freedom and for the freedom of us all.

However, whether we feel our circumstances dictate choosing invisibility or we have found the support to choose visibility, all of us have been affected by living in a homophobic world. Some of us carry old scars and some of us walk around with open wounds. I think of examples from my own life. Even though I think I am about as visible as I can be, what effect did it have on me to live invisibly for 16 years, terrified of being exposed and losing everything? Or after I was visible, to spend six months with my job and life threatened because as director of a county-wide system of Head Start programs I was said to have hired lesbians (true, two as cooks on a staff of 40) and to have said I was a lesbian and proud of it (false, though I wish I had)? Because I had not hid as a lesbian, I endured life-threatening phone calls, police harassment at my house, personnel committee meetings that I was not allowed to attend, and finally a large public hearing where I was made to stand outside while others went in to testify whether my being a lesbian affected my work. I survived this attack in large part because I was visible and because I had good supportive women around me. Those who led the attack were not primarily concerned with my lesbianism; they were looking for an opportunity to challenge my effectiveness and fire me. They mistakenly thought I would want to keep my sexual identity hidden and would be most vulnerable in that area. They also discovered that in the Arkansas Ozarks good character and ethics can sometimes have a greater impact than sexual identity.

But what does it do to a person to face that kind of hatred? How does it affect the woman whose parents say they would rather see her dead than a lesbian? The lesbian whom the judge calls an unfit mother and awards custody of her children to the father who is a known batterer? The young woman whose sister sends her weekly letters, each a sermon on the sin of homosexuality, accompanied by Bible verses and quotations from her fundamentalist preacher? The teenage girl who is jeered and called "dyke" by her classmates because she doesn't date and looks too "masculine"? The lesbian whose family has her kidnapped and who is raped repeatedly each day by her male kidnapper for deprogramming?

And then there are all of the covert forms of homophobia—the exclusion, the tolerance, the condescension, the subtle messages that lesbians are bad but you are the exception, the messages that just finding the right man would take care of the problem, the hints that this is just a phase and you will

hopefully outgrow it, the suggestions that lesbians live incomplete lives because wholeness lies in heterosexual relationships. What do these messages do to a lesbian's sense of self,
her sense of belonging in the world?

Lesbians, like people in all oppressed groups, have to work
on issues of self-esteem and self-worth to counter the damage
of internalized oppression faced by oppressed groups. Believ-
ing that we are inferior is what is known as internalized oppression. For instance, one of the weapons of racism is to pound
in relentlessly the messages that people of color aren't as smart,
as capable, as wise, as ambitious as white people. Hence, lesbians of color have to confront multiple oppressions and deal
with external/internalized homophobia, racism and sexism.
The messages that society gives lesbians and gay men are that
we are sick, immoral, destroyers of the family, abnormal, deviant, immature, etc. It is very, very difficult to grow up in the
midst of this constant bombardment and throw off all these
messages without internalizing any of them as true. Yet when
we do take them in, we do damage to ourselves and put severe
limits on our freedom to achieve everything we can be in
the world.

Though we are justified in our acknowledgement and response to external homophobia and often have little control
over it, we do have control over what we choose to internalize
as true. The challenge is to bring internalized homophobia to
consciousness, examine it, and set ourselves free from it.

We have to examine the impact it has had upon us to live
in a homophobic world and then take responsibility for our
own internalized homophobia and the way we present it to
the world. Too often, we do not make a distinction between
the legitimate danger of external homophobia and the times
when we could act with more freedom, the times when we im-
pose unnecessary restrictions upon ourselves. A test of ourselves is to look at how we behave when there is no apparent

external danger. Many newly identified lesbians tell stories about how when they were living heterosexual lives they were publicly affectionate with women but as soon as they recognized their lesbian identity, they would not show affection to women in those same public circumstances, even though their lesbian identity wasn't public and people still thought they were heterosexual. Where did that pressure for change in behavior come from? Others tell about how they don't show affection to their lovers even in public places such as airport waiting lounges where it is acceptable for people to show physical affection. Many of us can recall instances where we are touching hands over a restaurant table in a large city and when the waitress who neither knows us nor cares about us comes to the table, we quickly withdraw our hands.

These are minor examples, but they are telling because they show our fear carrying over to times when external danger is not apparent. And that's what we must review: how we behave with each other, with the public, how we think of ourselves, how we limit ourselves when we are in relatively safe places—the privacy of our homes, the lesbian community, etc. Internalized homophobia can impact every aspect of our lives and prohibit our growth and movement in the world. We must always remember that every piece of our internalized homophobia has its roots in external homophobia, and its purpose is to make us act against ourselves. Therefore, it is extremely important that we not blame ourselves for having taken in homophobia—to do so would be to give continued power to homophobia—but instead we must take strength and pleasure in our ability to exert control over our own lives by eliminating it.

Here are some of the ways internalized homophobia manifests itself in individuals and in our lesbian communities:

• *Isolation.* When homophobia can work to keep us isolated and separate from one another, its continued success is absolute. When there is a heavily enforced norm of compulsory heterosexuality, from our youngest days lesbians feel different, outside what is acceptable. Because fear keeps so many of us invisible, often this sense of being different joins with a sense of being the only one, making us individually feel there is something dreadfully wrong with me because I don't see others like me. Certainly there are not many visible lesbians for young lesbians to use as models. Feeling different and alone leads easily to the step of self-blame.

Early in the women's liberation movement, women saw isolation as an effective technique to keep us from working for our rights. Some of the very best work for liberation in the 1970s was finding ways to break silence on hard issues, to bring women out of isolation, and to bring us together in small groups to talk about our lives and in the process, to learn that our oppression, with its various faces, was the same. The women's movement broke the silence on rape, marital rape,

heterosexual battering, medical abuse of women, mastectomies, incest. The politicization of women came through gathering together in consciousness raising groups in the early days and in support groups later on to talk about our lives. These stories presented the common ground that broke isolation, and breaking isolation began breaking the power of sexism. In the 1980s, we have begun looking at racism, anti-Semitism, ageism, and ableism as other areas of common ground irrevocably connected to sexism.

Recently, I went to a lesbian and gay leadership weekend. On the first night we spent three hours telling our stories, focusing on what had brought us to be political activists. In each of those stories—each so different in urban and rural and religious and educational backgrounds—as each person told about the sense of being different, of confrontations with homophobia, I heard my own story. At that moment, it was disturbing to think of all the things that have kept lesbians and gay men separate from one another over the years. Our isolation from one another has prevented us from becoming an organized national movement.

• *Passing.* We do at least two kinds of passing. The first is to pass as heterosexuals in order to hide completely our lesbian identity, sometimes even going so far as to marry, live as part of a heterosexual family, etc. The second is be somewhat public as a lesbian but to pass through assuming "heterosexual dress and behavior" in order to be socially acceptable or "good lesbians." Because many of us have not seen enough strong, autonomous and successful lesbians, some lesbians work hard to gain acceptance through heterosexually approved behavior as a way to compensate for feeling an outsider. Then, when we begin to meet lesbians, we don't identify or bond with them, especially if they are not heterosexually acceptable, for we fear being thought to be like them or fear that through association with more visible lesbians, we will be known publicly as lesbians and will lose hard-won privilege. This same fear prevents us from particpating in lesbian social and political events, and from doing the things that build community and fight homophobia.

In our attempts to pass as heterosexuals, we cut ourselves off from other lesbians and add to our isolation. We feel that our acceptance by heterosexuals is conditioned upon their belief that we too are heterosexual, and consequently we never truly believe in their approval. Our self-esteem is damaged by the lies we have to tell in order to keep our identity secret, for we find no honor in our self-assessment as a dishonest person.

• *Self-hatred.* Self-hatred is a familiar corollary of isolation. If we take in and accept that we are sick, evil, deviants who hurt others by our very existence, then we can end up thinking we are not worthy of associating on an equal basis with others, both homosexual and heterosexual. Our self-blame instills a sense of inferiority. Low self-worth and self-esteem are great inhibitors of our potential: we either accept that we are not worthy of grace and love, of rights, and that we have to take whatever is offered us, no matter how inadequate, or we constantly have to prove to ourselves and others that we are worthy. Lack of a sense of self-worth makes us often accept the partial measure when we could demand the full measure.

• *Under-achievement.* A sense of not being worthy often limits what we ask of life. We see some lesbians working in jobs that require little of us because we think nothing else is possible for us. We accept low pay and little chance of advancement because we think we are not acceptable enough to apply for something greater. Instead of recognizing the standards of what is acceptable are at fault and challenging them, we accept limitations on our work and our growth. In self-protection, we sometimes work in jobs that don't call for a deep investment so that we won't be hurt if we should lose them for being a lesbian.

• *Over-achievement.* Just as we accept under-achievement, we often see lesbians virtually killing ourselves in our work in an effort to prove that we are good people. This same motivation drives many lesbians into the "helping" professions where one can demonstrate one's goodness and commitment to humanity. It's almost as if we think that if the end comes, if killing and imprisonment become widespread, those who have witnessed our demonstrated goodness will step forward to testify on our behalf and save us. We have the experience of Jews in Nazi Germany to prove to us that oppression does not work this way, that oppression does not care about one's essential goodness and good deeds; oppression is blind to all except its need to control people.

• *Physical health.* People have to think themselves worthy in order to be good to themselves in the care of their health. Often lesbians do not treat our bodies and physical health with kindness, perhaps because with our internalized homophobia we feel our bodies have betrayed us by having a sexual identity that is socially despised. We overfeed and underfeed our bodies and sometimes despise them, hiding them from the world in every way we can, dressing in ways that won't draw attention to the place where our spirit resides. We see the signs of low self-esteem in the way that some of us hold our bodies— the tightness, the rigidity, our shoulders up around our ears, our walking stiff-legged, our breasts held in defensively. We all suffer stress from living in a homophobic world, and those of us who choose to live invisibly suffer the additional stress of working to keep our identity secret. Our great, flowing energies get locked in our bodies, and the physical toll is great.

• *Mental health.* Lesbians struggling with identity in a homophobic world sometimes suffer chronic depression, feeling there is no way to reconcile who we are with the world at large. This sense of feeling trapped, of feeling a bad and worthless person can lead to suicide. Recent studies are beginning to show that many teenage suicides are connected to gay and lesbian issues of sexual identity. One can only wonder about teenagers' sense of self-worth in a world in which so many parents say, "I'd rather see you dead than a lesbian." Faced with extremes of isolation and ostracism, other lesbian and gay teenagers become runaways (or they are thrown away by their families), choosing instead to live the hard life of street people where they hope there is less judgment of who they are.

• *Alcohol and drug abuse.* There has been much discussion within the lesbian and gay community about our high rate of alcohol and drug abuse. Inasmuch as stress and low self-esteem can lead to abuse of the body, alcohol and drug abuse can be a major product of internalized homophobia. The combination of alcohol, drugs, and internalized homophobia creates a climate that fosters self-destruction. For many, alcohol and drugs are seen as a way to escape struggles with self and the world. Women who are predisposed to alcoholism receive little support not to drink from a social system that for many centers around lesbian bars, one of the few public places where lesbians feel safe to gather together.

• *Relationships with lovers/partners.* Because of our sense of being isolated in a hostile world, we often place undue expectations on our love relationships, assuming that the other person will fill all of our needs and it will be "the two of us against the world." Having no real safety in other places, we give our relationships a sanctity and importance that is larger than life. The other person becomes not only sanctuary but the buffer to the world's violence and the balm to all wounds. With so much importance placed upon the relationship, the slightest failure to meet expectations often becomes exaggerated and feels overwhelming. The disappointment becomes a source of betrayal and great pain. If the relationship is isolated, as many relationships are, especially among invisible lesbians, then what should be seen as a small problem in a broader perspective gets enlarged to the point that the relationship breaks down.

One of the concerns of the lesbian community is the brevity of love relationships. Among the many things that may contribute to unstable and brief relationships is our failure to recognize them as important. Because the heterosexual world does not honor lesbian relationships and offers no institutional or personal support for them, neither do many of us. Our relationships often struggle along against impossible odds: viewed by the world and many other lesbians as temporary and less consequential than heterosexual relationships; unsupported by lesbian or heterosexual institutions; lived in isolation and without many public models of success. There is probably more contemporary popular literature on heterosexual relationships (take a look at "women's" magazines, for one place) than on any other single subject and probably less on the subject of lesbian relationships than any other in lesbian literature. We can count on one hand the books that deal with lesbian relationships (unless one includes lesbian "romances"). Everywhere we turn, we get the message that our relationships are not important.

Those who live in large degrees of invisibility have even greater stress on their relationships. When one is invisible as a lesbian, she has to put all others before the relationship in order to protect it and herself. Consider these relationship stresses:

One person is invited to an office dinner or party but her lover cannot be included. Perhaps the occasion is in honor of the first person's work, yet her lover cannot participate. How does each feel?

One woman is going to visit her family for the holidays but she cannot take her lover with her. Or, if she does, the two of them must hide their relationship and act as though they are simply friends.

One woman's parents come to visit and prior to their arrival, the two lesbians hide all traces of their life together, trying to indicate they occupy separate bedrooms, putting away pictures of the two of them together, hiding their lesbian records and books, etc.

One woman becomes seriously ill and her family, as next of kin, is allowed to visit her in the hospital but her lover is not.

While walking on a beach and holding hands a thousand miles from home, two lesbians drop their hands as soon as they see a couple and a child coming toward them.

What messages do these small acts send a relationship? How is one to think the relationship is serious and important

if all others are put before it? It is only when we think our relationships are as valid as those of heterosexuals that they will
get the visibility and support necessary to thrive.

• *Lesbian battering.* When battered lesbians and other lesbians who work in the battered women's movement talked
about lesbian battering at the 1983 NCADV Violence in the
Lesbian Community Conference, we said that lesbian battering appears to be similar to heterosexual battering. That is,
it is caused by one exerting power and control over the other's
life. Our analysis also suggested that the similarity existed
not because, as some think, lesbians play roles and the one taking on a male role is the batterer, but because we as lesbians
learn violence and its methods from the heterosexual, male-
dominated world we grow up in. We went on to say that the
major difference between heterosexual battering and lesbian
battering is the impact of homophobia on the two individuals
in a lesbian relationship and on the relationship itself.

We have yet to understand fully the effect of internalized
homophobia upon lesbian battering, but we know from our
work in the battered women's movement that self-esteem issues play a large role. One of the things that happens early
in a woman's stay at a battered women's shelter is work on
self-esteem, the work that instills the deeply held belief that
no one deserves to be beaten. Given that lesbians have even
greater reason to experience low self-esteem than heterosexual women in that they suffer both sexism and homophobia,
we can infer that internalized homophobia has a significant
role in lesbians' response to battering.

• *Relationships with family and heterosexual friends.* Due
to homophobic attitudes held by our family and friends and
internalized homophobia on our own part, many of us do not
have authentic relationships with heterosexually identified
people. The greatest block is lack of openness. We often feel
that the love and acceptance we receive from family and friends

is conditional, that it is based on our being and acting according to prescribed ways, and that it will be withdrawn if we show much deviation from their expectations of us. Many of us have lived and continue to live in terror of someone we love finding out we are a lesbian and thereafter rejecting us. Because we think we cannot bear the loss of love and acceptance by our mother or father or sister or brother or best friend, we struggle to keep our lives secret from them. This fear of rejection always makes the relationships seem tenuous and at risk.

Because our family members or friends do not know we are lesbian, we are privy to their homophobic feelings that get expressed in our presence. Hearing their contempt for others, jokes about sissies and dykes and people with AIDS or whatever, we think we would be the focus of this painful contempt if they knew our sexual identity and all of our lives that grow from that source. As much as we want and need it, we never trust or believe in their love because we know they love only the socially acceptable person we present to them, not the complete self and life that we keep hidden. We cannot rest securely in that love.

Even when we don't know their attitudes, we often project what our families and friends would feel or do if they knew who we are; thus we keep from them any opportunity to be different or to change and grow. We convince ourselves that we know exactly what their response would be and we never take the risk that could bring forth an authentic relationship. By being invisible, we lose the possibility of developing understanding and support for lesbian sexual identity because we allow people's stereotypes and prejudices and limited understanding to remain in place when they don't realize they have lesbians and gay men in their families, in their churches, in their hospitals, in their work places. We cut off the possibility for their increased awareness and knowledge, and we lose allies for the struggle for gay and lesbian freedom.

• *Projection/protection.* We frequently develop an inordinate sense of responsibility for the well-being of our family and friends. We project what their responses to our lesbianism would be: I couldn't tell my mother (sister, friend, etc.) because it would kill her. Or it would just hurt her too much. Or it would make her worry about me all of the time. Or it would keep her in church praying for me. We not only project what their response might be but we go a step further in taking responsibility for their happiness, putting their good before our own. As we protect them from what we think is the killing or painful truth about ourselves, we prevent our lives and relationships from having wholeness. We also prevent them from having the opportunity to grow (and to overcome homophobia) by knowing the truth that lies in the diversity of people's lives.

Those of us who work in feminist organizations often do the same kind of thing: for the "good" of the organization, we keep our lives secret, asking ourselves how we can jeopardize this organization in the community by our visibility when it is already in jeopardy because it works on behalf of women. We sacrifice our rights, our wholeness, our health when our visibility would create the necessity for growth on the part of individuals and institutions. We have to recognize that what we are protecting loved ones and institutions from is their own homophobia.

Those who come from communities already under the attack of racism experience even greater conflict and pressure not to jeopardize further the community of color by exposing it to the additional attack of homophobia. Lesbians feel constant pressure to think of our oppression as insignificant compared to other oppressions.

Even when we have shared with loved ones that we are lesbian, many of us still withhold much of our lives in our daily interactions with them. The success of internalized homophobia is to make us think that our lives are not as valid or as important as those of heterosexuals. Hence, when they are discussing babies and husbands and the daily events and circumstances of their heterosexual lives, we don't always put forth the details of our lives. Old fears keep us protecting ourselves.

These relationships lack authenticity, wholeness. The major impact of internalized homophobia upon our relationships is our inability to believe ourselves worthy of authentic relationships. We settle for the half-filled glass, not expecting for ourselves the full portion. In workshops, I often ask groups to list the components of authentic relationships, and almost always the first thing listed is honesty, followed by trust. In varying order are equality, open communication and affection, autonomy, respect, safety, interdependence, love, considerateness, humor, etc. While admitting we haven't seen many examples of authentic relationships among heterosexuals, we say that most of us as lesbians are blocked in our relationships by the first two: honesty and trust. If we cannot share the major portion of our being with those we love, then how can we hope for authenticity? And the lack of authenticity increases our sense of isolation.

• *Horizontal oppression/hostility.* One of the places we have witnessed the most damage from internalized homophobia is within our own lesbian communities. It is here that internalized homophobia does its most successful work among all oppressed people to prevent unity and growth in our social and political interactions. Suffering the pain and damage of a world that despises us, we transform our pain into anger and turn it against one another instead of at the source of oppression. Instead of focusing that anger and energy in a unified way to make the changes needed in the dominant culture, where it is more risky and dangerous to confront oppression, we expend ourselves attacking and limiting one another. We become the harshest and most exacting critics of lesbian lives.

Perhaps because there is so little safety in the world, we

81

yearn for the comfort of being accepted in our own communities. This yearning can become distorted into a fear of differences and lead us to have little tolerance for those who hold different political views or lead different lifestyles. It then becomes ironic that it is our very longing for a place of safety that leads us to create a place that is safe only for the few who think and act and look alike. We divide along lines of political correctness, lifestyles, class issues, race, degrees of passing and acceptability, separatism, inclusiveness, etc. Our organizing within the lesbian and gay movements gets blocked by anger and personal attacks as the pain we have experienced at the hands of the world works itself out against our own in this setting. When these conflicts happen and people get hurt even more deeply, no one feels victorious because there is no satisfaction over having achieved power over others; instead, the victory goes to the homophobic world because we are left with a greater sense of isolation and exclusion. We have deepened despair because we feel if there is no place, no safety and peace to be found within our own communities, our own organizations where we are in charge of creating new ways to live, then there seems little hope of safety and peace anywhere. From a climate of despair and increased isolation it is difficult to find the hope and will to bring about the interconnectedness that is the basis of organizing for freedom.

## Setting Ourselves Free

For lesbians to experience freedom, individually and collectively, we have to free ourselves both from within and without. Freedom does not come from the struggles of a few leaders in isolation: Gandhi did not free Indians by the strength of his single will, just as Martin Luther King did not bring increased freedom to black citizens through solitary efforts. Great strides for freedom come when large groups of oppressed people come to believe that they *deserve* freedom and then

82

work together to achieve it. In our history, those who have power and control over other groups of people have not been known to give it up suddenly and willingly out of the goodness of their hearts: power has been reshaped and redistributed through the growing strength and demands of the oppressed.

As long as lesbians as a people do not think ourselves worthy of the rights and freedoms accorded those who are heterosexually identified, then our work toward social change for lesbians holds little hope for success. In every great social change movement of this century, people who were despised took extraordinary risks to resist oppression and to make clear to the world their essential worth and common humanity. From the Untouchables in India to the very poorest black people in the United States, people have risked their lives in the face of the weapons of hatred. They began with small risks and took on larger ones as they grew stronger in their faith in the righteousness of their cause, and that faith grew from working together in groups that discovered the commonness of their individual experiences. That interconnection in which even the poorest and most wretched were considered equally precious in the pursuit of freedom provided the spiritual basis for the movement. Each movement was inclusive of all who shared any part of the oppression.

Though lesbians have grown in visibility over the past twenty years, great numbers of our population still live in complete or partial invisibility. Through the creation of lesbian institutions and culture, we have done significant work on lesbian self-esteem and pride. However, much is underground work and is enjoyed by women only in the privacy of their homes or by women who allow themselves visibility only at all-lesbian gatherings for music festivals, concerts, etc. In terms of visibility within the dominant culture, there has not been as much success or impact.

For many of us, then, becoming entirely visible is the central place of risk taking. It is also at the core of our self-esteem and organizing issues. When we talk about the necessity of becoming visible in our sexual identity, it would be a mistake to assume facilely that every woman faces equal risks and thereby insist that we all employ the same strategies and methods in coming out. The circumstances of our lives differ. While visibility for one woman might mean the loss of a job, for another it might mean the loss of her children, and for another the loss of her life. Certainly risks differ for lesbians of color and white lesbians. We cannot ignore these differences by insisting that everyone reach the same place at the same time in the same way. What we can ask of ourselves, however, is that each of us continuously push the limits of our safety in our risk taking: that we not be content with each level of visibility but keep moving ourselves forward to freedom. Each of us can set personal freeing goals. From these individual efforts will come group movement.

Until we lose the fear of visibility, we will not be able to succeed in our movement building, for we will not have the numbers required to make an impact on public opinion or policy, because women will not have the courage to come to meetings or take public stands. And visible lesbians will continue to be unable to identify their lesbian sisters even to invite them to join the movement. We will not know our potential non-lesbian allies because they will continue to be unable to recognize their lesbian co-workers, relatives, and friends. When fundamentalist ministers preach damning sermons about homosexuals, lead campaigns for the elimination of gay and lesbian teachers and of books that mention homosexuality, and suggest quarantine and camps for people with AIDS, their audiences will agree because they mistakenly think they have never known a homosexual except those presented in the media. For many years, the lesbian and gay movement has speculated about the impact it would make if on one specified day every one who was lesbian or gay wore a lavender armband and did not work that day. We think the work of many institutions would be seriously impaired or stopped that day, and all those who had assumed we were heterosexuals would be forced to rethink their views of homosexuals.

Every act of lesbian visibility is an act of resistance. Its defiance says no to the oppression of homophobia. There are lesbians throughout the world who bravely perform these acts of resistance every day, and even the smallest act has an impact upon our individual lives and upon society. For their bravery some women gain a larger breathing space in the world while others suffer terrible reprisals. Our experiences have taught us that it is important to develop support among our friends and allies for these acts so that we are not destroyed by them. As we develop this support for our freeing actions, we break isolation and begin the steps of becoming a movement.

Each successful step toward visibility develops self-esteem and pride and strengthens us for the next step. One of the ways we have found to develop our sense of connectedness and our self-esteem is through the telling of our individual stories. The telling of these stories provides our understanding of our common experience, the basis for an analysis of oppression, and brings us out of our isolation. Our stories help us reclaim our history as a people, a history that brings us pride. What we have learned from other freedom movements, as well as from the beginning of our own, is that there are not just some stories that must be heard, but that all the stories are of equal importance and must be heard. There are not acceptable and unacceptable stories or people. As we build this movement, we must include all of us or face the failure that comes from building a new movement for freedom on an old system of oppression.

The telling of our stories, the sharing of our lives through all our many diverse voices is the strong foundation of our movement building and it is available to all of us, whether rural or urban, old or young, whatever our circumstance, for the best work for building support for our identities is done in small groups that can be organized by any eight to ten women and held in private homes. The most empowering groups are led by group members, not a professional facilitator. These consciousness raising/action groups were the backbone of the women's movement in the early 1970s. There are simple steps to follow: inclusion of all voices, respectful listening, agreed upon confidentiality, support, focus on a certain subject or period in life, and then reflection upon common themes and meaning. There are few experiences that offer so much potential for connection and wholeness as do successful groups. Over the weeks of meeting together we learn that we are capable of presenting and analyzing our own lives, that we are not alone in our experiences, and that we hold within ourselves our own answers and capacity for being in charge of our lives. Finally, we learn that our stories hold important and universal truths.

For the elimination of internalized homophobia and the development of a strong movement we need at least three kinds of groups: consciousness raising—support groups—and political action groups—and all can be organized within our homes or within our women's organizations. Consciousness raising groups are usually general and wide reaching in their themes, covering all aspects of women's lives and developing political analysis from the content of women's stories. Support groups most often focus on a specific issue that is explored and analyzed: lesbian mothers, chemical dependency, lesbian battering, relationships, survivors of rape or incest, etc. Political action groups are organized to respond to homophobic institutions and actions and involve planning and carrying out strategies for change.

To be most effective, each kind of group should carry elements of all three: consciousness raising, support, and political action. Let's use the example of lesbian battering. Although the battered women's movement has begun work on the issue of lesbian battering, it is clear to lesbians both within and without the movement that a joint effort is needed between the lesbian community and the battered women's movement because until battered women's shelters address homophobia, they cannot work satisfactorily with battered lesbians. Yet the experience of workers in the battered women's movement, especially lesbians, is valuable and necessary in approaching the problem. In facing this dilemma, many people are choosing to develop support groups within the lesbian community and then to involve workers from the battered women's movement. These groups begin with women sharing their stories of the violence they have experienced at the hands of their female partners, giving support for each woman's pain and struggle and validating her experience, discussing common themes and analyzing the causes, and then developing strategies for creating safe homes and doing training on homophobia and lesbian battering for shelters so that battered lesbians have places to go for safety. Such a group would use all three elements: consciousness raising, support, and political action.

Developing such community groups has a number of positive benefits: they bring us together, enable us to be connected, demonstrate that we are authorities in our lives, and heighten our sense of individual and community self-worth as we learn that we can find ways to solve our problems. This work is movement building at its most basic and fundamental level. It is also central to our very survival because in an overtly homophobic world, no other institutions or individuals are going to do this work for us in ways that affirm us as positive human beings.

From the support groups, we come together for the larger community connections, work, and visibility. Though this is an area where so very much more work needs to be done, we have many models of successful organizing to develop ways for lesbians to come together in enjoyable, positive ways as communities that work on their problems and have pride. A few of them:

• In a very conservative city in the south central United States, there is a collective of 12 women who (without funding) operate a storefront bookstore, sponsor workshops and conferences, hold a women's retreat at least once a year, operate a coffee house, hold frequent potluck dinners, produce women's concerts, and publish a monthly newsletter that goes out to over 700 women in the area.

• In another city in the same area there is a lesbian supper club that meets every Saturday night at various previously designated restaurants.

• Another alternative to bars is the coffee house in a city in the upper midwest where women can come for conversation and music and poetry without having to face alcohol and a smoky room.

• A group in the northeast does social organizing for new and longtime lesbians in their university town. A group meets once every month and sets the calendar of events for that month—such as potluck dinners, gatherings at designated restaurants for brunch, volleyball games, gatherings to watch special sports events at someone's home, etc.—and then they leave the schedule with the gay and lesbian switchboard so that everyone can have access to the information simply by calling in. A special feature of this organizing is that each month the chair of the last month shares her role with a new chair who will then conduct the meeting the next month with a new chair, and so on, enabling everyone to learn and share leadership.

• In a city in the northwest there is a lesbian community building project that organized a conference to examine the makeup of the lesbian community, to analyze its needs, and to work on strategies for strengthening it. This project is ongoing as a growing group of women look at the overall needs of the community and provide information about all of the events, services, etc., available to lesbians.

• In a Rocky Mountain state there is a lesbian outdoor club that organizes groups of women once a month for hiking trips, backpacking, whitewater canoeing, bicycling, etc.

• In a small southern city, there is a volunteer gay and lesbian switchboard that helps lesbians and gay men find services, community events, and places to meet people.

• In a major midwestern city, there is a lesbian organization that offers support groups for battered lesbians, lesbian mothers, older lesbians, etc., and sponsors workshops, coffee houses, cultural events.

These are only a few examples. There are now women's music festivals in every region of the country, a midwestern women's festival (not focused on music) that has a ten-year history, a lesbian retreat in the south that has been going on for six years, a ten-year lesbian writers camp in the south, as well as numerous other festivals, retreats, camps, and conferences throughout the country. There is the Metropolitan Community Church as well as groups affiliated with mainline churches such as Affirmation with the United Methodist Church and Dignity with the Catholic Church, and groups that meet to discuss, develop and live women's spirituality. There are lesbian counseling centers, and groups that do co-counseling and peer counseling. There are lesbian task forces or caucuses connected to many national organizations such as the National Coalition Against Domestic Violence and the National Association Against Sexual Assault. (It should be noted, however, that almost all of these resources are all white or white dominated; lesbians of color have far fewer options.) A notable institution for lesbians of color is the Kitchen Table Press. A strong political group is the National Coalition of Black Lesbians and Gays. There are newspapers and magazines and books and movies about our lives. And there are groups and individuals around the country who do public education on homophobia. Each example acts in resistance to homophobia and for the survival of lesbians as an integral and valid part of our culture.

And each is not yet enough. We have done our best work in developing a lesbian culture and in creating organizations to address our needs, but these have had their greatest effect upon people who live in large cities. Still, large numbers of lesbians live in isolation, untouched by our organizations. Also we have extensive work to do on inclusiveness, on our recognition of the value of every lesbian, on discovering ways to give lesbians equal voice, especially for those who have traditionally been unrecognized by the dominant white, middleclass culture. We have to eliminate our own barriers to freedom.

But the place where we have to do the greatest work is in the area of action for change in the public arena. We are at the point in our growth as a movement where we must be involved in the kind of political action that requires visibility. We must present our issues in public forums concerning subjects that affect us. We cannot accept the invisibility imposed from without and within. When there are discussions about violence against women, incarceration, housing, childcare, physical and mental healthcare, criminal justice responses, religious and spiritual needs, education, etc., we must present our issues, make our presence known as a part of every community. We must be seen and heard and read in the mass media, not just within our own.

Our actions have to be directly defiant of and resistant to oppression through the techniques of nonviolence learned from other movements. This work will involve boycotts, marches, fasts, vigils, noncooperation with oppression. Much of our work now requires patient training for political action through the development of a mass movement that recognizes as its allies all other oppressed people. It will not be a movement in isolation from people of color, poor people, old people, differently abled people, people from third world countries, women everywhere, and gay men. Our movement will be simply our part of this larger movement for freedom, and as we go forward we will develop awareness of our connectedness with this larger movement and our responsibility to other oppressed people. We will recognize that we all go forward together or ultimately not at all.

Of necessity, our commitment to social change is for the long term. We do not expect overnight success nor an easy gift of freedom. We will live as we are now learning to live: in recognition that every step we take must be a conscious step for liberation for all of us.

# Afterword:
# Where We Are Now

SINCE 1988, WHEN I WROTE *Homophobia: A Weapon of Sexism*, there have been dramatic changes in the lives of lesbian, gay, bisexual and transgendered people. There have also been dramatic changes in my own life which mirror some of the struggles of this movement. When I wrote *Homophobia*, I was working for the Women's Project in Arkansas (as I am now) and, in addition to my work at home, traveling the country doing homophobia and racism workshops for a battered women's movement that was vibrant and well organized. While on a two-month sabbatical, I wrote the book in an isolated cabin in the mountains of Arkansas, thinking I would take it to a copy store to have copies made to send to battered women's programs, churches, community organizations, and educational institutions where I had presented workshops. Instead, with the help of Chardon Press, a publisher for non-profit organizations, it became a "real" book, used by individuals, organizations and educators, with its profits providing a source of funding for the Women's Project's on-going work. The book was completed just before the Women's Project began its Women's Watchcare Network that monitors racist, religious, sexist, and anti-gay and lesbian violence, as well as the activities of the racist far right and the theocratic right (those whose agenda is to merge church and state). This new project plunged me into the middle of direct response to this country's right wing.

Seven years later, in 1995, I sat in a cabin on the coast of Oregon to write a second book, *In the Time of the Right: Reflections on Liberation*, in a time when battered women's programs were more professionalized and institutionalized but less organized, and when lesbian and gay issues had been given exposure through every form of media and brought into the homes of virtually everyone in this country. My work on the right in Arkansas brought me to the attention of the Lesbian Community Project and the Coalition for Human Dignity in Oregon at the beginning of an attack from the Oregon Citizen's Alliance (OCA). They called me there to work with them to help people understand that the OCA's anti-gay and lesbian ballot measure was, in fact, an attempt to dismantle civil rights and an attack on democracy itself.

And now, in 1997, having moved to Oregon where the right continues its activities with an anti-government, anti-worker, anti-tax agenda, I return to *Homophobia* to try to give some accounting of what has happened since its publication. I still find that my work centers on homophobia and racism, though with much more emphasis on economic injustice. The issues remain the same but the context is different, for the size and power of the organized right have grown exponentially, along with the domination of people's economic lives by the maneuvering of corporations.

What seemed like complicated issues of homophobia and sexism in 1988 have become even more complex, and we have experienced extraordinary successes and failures in our efforts to dismantle these two oppressions. Now, nine years later, readers have asked me to analyze some of the major issues that have been raised during the intervening time. To do so would require another book, so I have chosen instead to frame some concerns about homophobia and sexism as they appear in today's new context for the reader's further investigation and analysis, and to provide a short bibliography for more extended discussion of the issues raised here.

Once a book is written, it becomes a marker for the historical moment, and thereafter we can use it for assessing changes that have occurred since its publication. For example, in *Homophobia*, I consistently refer to lesbians and gay men and never to bisexual and transgendered people, though I write at length about the need to transform gender roles. Now, thanks to organizing and education by the latter two groups (and in particular by youth activists), building on the gender analysis of radical feminists of the 1970s who envisioned a gender-free world, we are coming to understand that our goal is not just sexual liberation or the elimination of homophobia and sexism. We now also seek the gender liberation that brings freedom to all.

This understanding, which has widened the scope of our politics, has mandated more inclusive and descriptive language. For the purposes of this afterword, I will often use "lgbt?" to stand for lesbians, gay men, bisexuals, transsexuals, transgendered, and questioning people. As youth activists have taught us, the *question mark* in this list is particularly important because it provides an opening for a broader range of people to enter, and it indicates that we do not yet have all the answers on sexual and gender identity. However, I will also use the word "queer" to describe the same community of people. In this country, it is indeed queer to be outside the dominant paradigm, and we can embrace the word and its political implication of resistance and change as an honored designation on the road to liberation. By the time we reach that place where there is no longer a dominant two-gender paradigm, with the oppression that accompanies it, we hopefully will have evolved new language to describe ourselves as one common humanity embracing large and small, ever-changing differences.

Of the many changes that have occurred in our lives, I want to focus on some major ones that have been brought about by the organizing of the theocratic right and also on those which have occurred internally within the queer movement. From these brief "snapshots" of our time, perhaps we can draw political lessons and understanding.

## Two threats from the right

The right's attacks against the lesbian and gay community have a long history, but their increased vehemency in the 1990s

95

occurred within the context of escalating economic and social chaos. As corporations downsized, cut benefits, moved production out of the country, and workers suffered loss of jobs and salaries, the right moved to organize people around their fears and discontent. Directing our attention away from the extraordinary increases in wealth for corporations, CEOs, and stockholders, they sent us messages that traditionally oppressed groups (people of color, women, lesbians and gay men, poor people) were the cause of the country's woes. Indeed, they promoted a sense of scarcity (there isn't enough to go around) and meanspiritedness (someone is going to take from you what is rightfully yours). The combination of these messages and people's fears created fertile ground for highly organized scapegoating directed toward the very people who are fighting for equality.

The right has used homophobia, sexism, and racism as the magnetic fields for organizing heterosexuals, men, and white people to oppose civil rights and democratic values. It has organized middle and working class people around anti-tax and anti-government sentiment, leading to an attack against services for the poor and increased economic injustice.

One of the right's strategies was to overtly organize heterosexuals around their homophobia while covertly moving their racist agenda. Some 15 years after the right's first major public attack against homosexuals (the Anita Bryant campaign), it launched its full artillery in 1992 with anti-gay ballot initiatives in Oregon and Colorado which were designed to use homophobia as a vehicle for dismantling civil rights for all oppressed groups. In these ballot measures, the right carefully equated civil rights with "special rights;" linked them to "minority status," affirmative action and quotas; and asserted that civil rights should be "deserved," based on good behavior, and put to a popular vote. By linking the civil rights of lesbians and gay men to language associated with race ("special rights," "minority status," "affirmative action," "quotas"), the right led many white people and heterosexuals of all races to join together to redefine civil rights and their application. (It is no surprise that major anti-affirmative action and anti-immigrant campaigns sprang up the following year.)

While the right used its large institutions and organized constituency to move a massive anti-gay media campaign, the lesbian, gay, bisexual, transgender community and its allies rose up in the largest display of collective power that it had ever known. People raised large amounts of money for electoral campaigns; they wrote articles, letters and op ed pieces; they provided public education in every possible arena; they organized rallies, marches and cultural events; and they came out in droves, talking to friends, families, co-workers, and strangers about their lives and their humanity.

Ballot Measure 9 was defeated in Oregon, Amendment 2 won in Colorado (later to be declared unconstitutional by the U.S. Supreme Court), and we experienced both victories and defeats in the flurry of local and state ballot initiatives that followed, as the right reorganized to launch local attacks.

## What was gained

• The queer community gained visibility to a degree that would have taken dozens of years to achieve. As the right attacked us in its publications, talked about us in its churches, radio and television programs, and made the nature of our humanity public debate all over the country, they simultaneously helped us develop a public consciousness of queer life and helped introduce and accustom people to our existence in their midst. In response to their dis/misinformation, we found the opportunity to present our own truth, and in ways small and large there has been an explosion of information at every level of society.

• Thousands of people who had never been politically active joined in these defensive campaigns and developed political experience and skills. We became an electoral presence as candidates for office, as voters, and as fundraisers.

• We discovered and created new allies. Most were gained from the new visibility of queers: family, friends, co-workers. The development of allies in social change organizations, where queer leadership had so often been closeted or quiet about queer issues, was especially welcomed. Some of these organizations, having gained an awareness of queer oppression, now put our issues on their agendas and supported open, visible queers in leadership.

• Because of the right's salacious videotapes and negative images of transgendered persons, people living with AIDS, and S/M practitioners, there was motivation for these targeted constituencies to organize more intensely, offering the queer community a leading, radical edge of gender and sexual analysis that provides a vision of liberation that is expansive and inclusive.

• The right's ballot initiatives helped us understand their larger agenda: to dismantle civil rights, introduce authoritarianism and replace democracy with theocracy—government by rulers claiming divine sanction from, in this case, a (white) Christian god. Also, as we experienced an attack of the ferocity common in the lives of other oppressed groups, more of us came to a clearer understanding of the connection among oppressions. This understanding has led some activists to a far broader commitment to multi-racial and multi-issue politics and to the creation and defense of participatory democracy.

## The down side

• In order to gain public approval, many people adopted the strategy of "mainstreaming," presenting the queer movement as white, middle class, and family-oriented, different only in same gender sexual partners. A common expression became "We are just like everyone else;" its theme was "Our place at the table." Terrified of association with "fringe elements"—such as queers of color, bisexuals, sex radicals such as the leather and S/M communities, transgendered and transsexual persons, the homeless and poor—the proponents of a mainstream agenda fostered divisions within our own movement as they sought the status quo of a heterosexual society. This strand of the movement became focused on the pursuit of the privileges of serving in the military and of getting legally married.

While wanting and fighting for equality in these areas is a necessary part of the achievement of our full civil rights, wanting them with no analysis of what the institutions represent and/or perpetuate, and of the many who get left out of those privileges is destructive and divisive. Some of the greatest damage done by a mainstream agenda is the further marginalization of those already marginal in the community. Many of us are unable or unwilling to serve in the military and thus gain its benefits. Many of us do not want to marry: those who do not have partners, those who prefer relationships alternative to long-term monogamy, or the lesbians who have seen marriage as an institution used to keep women restricted and oppressed. The goal of mainstreaming is too narrow. While we need just laws that recognize our relationships, it is also critical that we fight for every individual to have universal health care and education, a safe job with a livable wage, and a healthy and safe environment.

• In the midst of discovering and creating new allies, there was also harm done to potential alliances, in particular within the civil rights community when white individuals, speaking on behalf of the lgbt? movement, compared this movement of the 1980s and 1990s to the 1960s Civil Rights Movement. The queer movement, which failed to help create and support the inclusion and leadership of queers of color, now stood on shaky ground as it tried to present itself to black communities as a multi-racial movement for "civil rights for everyone." Its classism, which had gloried in a marketing firm's faulty research suggesting that queers were predominantly well-to-do, heavily consuming, and worthy of being targeted by advertising, now presented difficulties when comparing lgbt? people to African Americans who suffered from exploitation and poverty both before and after the gains of the Civil Rights Movement. In too many instances we called for other movements to support us in the face of attack when our own racism and classism had prevented us from an organized or visible history of institutional support for anyone else's struggles or more than a cursory knowledge of their issues.

• While fighting the ballot measures, we did not use this opportunity well to build the queer institutions in our local communities. The queer community and its allies raised millions of dollars to defeat these ballot measures and to carry out legal strategies. Meanwhile, many queer organizations suffered from serious financial problems. Also, the leadership and activists who emerged during the campaigns often did not move from them into on-going local organizing for the longer struggle for liberation. Many local queer organizations are now struggling for leadership and, ultimately, for survival.

## A more subtle and complex approach by the right

After the defeat of Ballot Measure 9 in Oregon and the U.S. Supreme Court's decision that Colorado's Amendment 2 was unconstitutional, the theocratic right diversified its approach to controlling lesbians, gay men, bisexuals, transgendered people, and women. It began to move out of the electoral arena and focus on state legislatures (with the Defense of Marriage Act, anti-choice laws), as well as local government via school and library boards (sex education, censorship), and city councils (anti-discrimination ordinances, public funding). It launched an all-out campaign against those people who had fought to gain equal rights and access to opportunity. In an effort to unravel civil rights and liberties, it focused on attacks against feminism, lgbt? civil rights and marriage, welfare, immigration, affirmative action, taxation, school choice, the First Amendment, and crime. Having learned how to fight anti-queer ballot initiatives, we in the lgbt community suddenly found ourselves scrambling to keep up with changes in tactics.

100

When the right introduced its anti-choice campaigns in the 1980s and its ballot initiatives in the 1990s, most people sensed its political power. Organizations such as Focus on the Family, the Traditional Values Coalition, and the American Family Association backed these campaigns and grew in strength as they built a constituency around the idea that the breakdown of the family was caused by sexual freedom. However, while the spotlight has been on these groups, little attention has been given to the extraordinary growth of Promise Keepers, the mass Christian men's movement that many authorities who analyze the right believe poses a much more devastating threat to the freedom of the lgbt? community and women, as well as the country as a whole. It is here that sexism and homophobia quietly join to motivate hundreds of thousands of men "to take this country for Christ." Promise Keepers presents a style of organizing that is difficult to counter because its use of mass media and mass psychology to present "good" messages of men's responsibility and commitment masks its subtext of training for domination. It represents a strategic change for the right.

Founded by former University of Colorado football coach, Bill McCartney, a primary backer of Amendment 2, Promise Keepers has grown in five years to 1.2 million men, a staff of 400, and an $115 million annual budget. It is backed by Christian right leadership such as James Dobson of the powerful Focus on the Family and Pat Robertson of the Christian Coalition—both rabidly anti-gay. Its mission statement tells us that "Promise Keepers is a Christ-centered ministry dedicated to uniting men through vital relationships to become godly influences in their world."

Built on a military model, PK organizes through local churches to bring men together in large rallies held in football stadiums around the country. They then return home to meet in small groups, led by "key men," who are coordinated through "ambassadors." Its membership is over 95% white, cuts across all economic classes, is both rural and urban, and is also currently organizing in prisons.

101

Why should we be concerned about a movement of men who are being encouraged to take more responsibility in their families and their communities? The problem is not that Promise Keepers are Christians, led by fundamentalist Christians, nor that they are all men (although many women have good reasons to be nervous about sports stadiums full of men singing and chanting and doing "the wave" together). The problem is the ideology that promotes authoritarianism and patriarchal "family values." Their rapidly growing constituency, trained in obedience and domination, has the capacity to be the ground troops that fight the battle for the merger of church and state.

Promise Keepers promote domination, referred to in the milder term of "leadership," over those who are not male and not Christian. An often quoted example is the statement by Tony Evans in *Seven Promises of a Promise Keeper*:

*I can hear you saying, "I want to be a spiritually pure man. Where do I start?"*

*The first thing you do is sit down with your wife and say something like this: "Honey, I've made a terrible mistake. I've given you my role. I gave up leading this family, and I forced you to take my place. Now I must reclaim that role."*

*Don't misunderstand what I am saying here. I'm not suggesting that you ask for your role back, I'm urging you to take it back. If you simply ask for it, your wife is likely to say, "Look, for the last ten years, I've had to raise these kids, look after the house, and pay the bills. I've had to get a job and still keep up my duties in the home. I've had to do my job and yours. You think I'm just going to turn everything back over to you?"*

Promise Keepers has attracted men who feel that society is falling apart; men who are angry at women; men who feel that they have lost power to women and minorities; men who have lost jobs and/or the ability to provide well economically for their families; and men who want to be more whole and have greater purpose. While there is much to appreciate in their exhorting men to take more responsibility in their families and communities, there is much to be concerned about in their fundamentalist leaders' anti-feminist, anti-queer, authoritarian views that provide a subtext for all of their organizing. This is key to understanding how they work: the subtext is as powerful as their overt exhortations to be "men of integrity." One could go to a Promise Keeper rally and never hear the word "homosexual" but in the product sales tent there are large displays of materials from groups such as Exodus International who work to convert queers to heterosexuality. And in the sermons men are told they should not be "sissy men" but "manly" followers of Christ. As women and queers, we can never ignore that Promise Keepers organize around heterosexual male power—and the word "equality" is never spoken.

Deterred perhaps by its popular appeal, few feminist, queer, or progressive organizations have successfully challenged the Promise Keepers, though organizations such as the National Gay and Lesbian Task Force have done an admirable job of creating public education packets and helping local groups develop strategies. Many think that PK is the organization that can be the cornerstone in the success of the right's agenda to merge church and state and to establish fundamentalist Christian authoritarianism that rejects any deviation from patriarchal values. This is what we have to be prepared for—not just the overt attacks by the Right, but the larger forces, whose agenda is more subtle and covert, that can move people and messages to threaten our very being. To challenge this mass movement will require strategic alliance work between queers, progressive white men, women of all races, people of faith, and men of color.

## The struggle for alliances and multi-issue politics

One fault line in our movement has been the failure of men, and particularly white gay men, to make alliances with women of all genders and sexualities. Heterosexual women were our best allies and voters in the ballot measure campaigns. And while lesbians have been a major source of institutional and personal support in the AIDS movement, few gay men have openly and collectively supported feminist concerns. If, indeed, homophobia and sexism are inextricably connected, it is imperative that gay men work against sexism. And it follows that if homophobia and sexism are connected because of gender oppression, it is vital that heterosexual women, lesbians, and gay men connect with and support the liberation of bisexual and transgendered people.

Another fault line is that concentration on single-issue "identity" politics (the bringing together of people who share a single common identity such as sexual orientation, gender or race) has led many lesbians and gay men to promote a narrow, white middle-class agenda. The failure to integrate race and class analysis into our political strategies and the failure to identify with race and class struggles has led many "mainstream" queers to isolate themselves from people of color and poor people within our movement. If people are not included and linked *within* our movement, it follows that we cannot connect with them as allies in other movements. The problem is not that queers of color and poor queers are absent from our movement; it is that the most prominent, *funded* leadership is white and middle-class. Such is our public face, and such are the identified issues we are asked to support. To those in other struggles, we appear to lack integrity because, acting in accordance with the dominant powers, we exclude those who do not fit a defined norm. Our movement often seems to be one designed to increase the comfort and privilege of those who already have the greatest access to opportunity. If we are willing to marginalize members of our own community because of their race, class or sexuality, how can we be trusted by those we seek as allies?

It is these fault lines that have divided our movement, impeding its progress. The right has used them successfully to diminish the general public's support of our efforts for liberation.

IN THE LATE 1990s, there are several key areas where we find ourselves defending our positions from the attack by the right: civil rights, the equal right to marry, non-discrimination in employment and the military. On the surface, all of these issues appear broad and inclusive. However, I believe the argument for them has been from a privileged gay perspective, not from an inclusive, liberation perspective. Here are a few brief examples:

• As a movement, we have failed to make the case that the goal is civil rights for all, not just the few, and to make alliances with others seeking civil rights. In our presentations to the public through the media, with the notable exception of the National Gay and Lesbian Task Force, our organizations have not taken a firm stand on civil rights issues related to immigration or affirmative action or abortion rights or on the criminalization of poor people and loss of due process. Often our leaders have insisted upon comparing our struggles to the Civil Rights Movement of the 1960s rather than insisting that we need to join in that movement's continued struggles today.

• The issue of the equal right to marry gives us an ideal opportunity to make alliances with women who have struggled through three waves of the women's movement to analyze and change the institution of marriage. Instead, the primary argument has been "If heterosexuals have it, then we deserve it, too." Rather than asserting that we want to be just like heterosexuals, we perhaps should be asking just what it is the right is fighting so hard to protect and maintain. The mad rush to pass the Defense of Marriage Act should be a signal to us that marriage is an important linchpin in the right's world view of patriarchal hierarchy. Certainly, that world view has been the underpinning of oppression of women and queers. The issue of the equal right to marry can open up the full discussion of this question: What would happen to gender oppression if there were no state-sanctioned marriage? A look at some of the nurturing and supportive relationships and families that we as queers have developed outside the paradigm of marriage points to a whole range of options beyond the right's "traditional family" structure of exclusivity and dominance.

• Again, the debate over "gays" in the military has offered a chance to make alliances with women, poor people, and people of color. As with civil rights, one of the primary arguments has been "We are just like blacks were in the 1940s—they got their right to serve, we want ours." It is true that there are some similarities (the major one being the drive to maintain the status quo of dominance through discrimination), but much of what stands at the center of the objection to queers is sexual difference, sexual threat, and sexual confusion. The struggle queers face in gaining equality in the military is virtually the same that women face. It is the battle of "non-traditional jobs," and it is both economic and social. The arguments against women and queers are echoes of each other: "We can't have you here because you would ruin morale." "We can't promise you safety." "Your presence would cause sexual trouble." "You can't do the work of 'real men'." "We can't have you using the same bathrooms." "You can't share tight quarters such as on a ship." It is important, also, to note how homophobia doubly affects women in the military—lesbians tend to be discharged faster, and any woman who rejects male advances or harassment can easily be accused of lesbianism and suffer humiliation, threats, and sometimes violence.

What is lacking in mainstream gay analysis of the U.S. military is its gender discrimination, its role in economic opportunity for poor people, and its role as an imperialist force. There are many allies to be made among people in struggle with the military.

• Many people have been supportive of the effort to end employment discrimination because it is proactive rather than reactive, offers a chance to do work that cuts across class and race, and has broad popular support. However, much of the attention has been focused on working with queer employee groups within corporations rather than with queer trade unionists organized within the unions as "lavender labor" groups. It has been difficult to gain support for a political strategy regarding people who work low-paid, low-profile jobs. Again, this issue seems one that provides an opportunity to link queer discrimination with discrimination based on race, sex, age, and physical ability.

Our goal has to be to eliminate discrimination in the workplace for *everyone*, not just queers. This calls for looking at vehicles by which discrimination can be eliminated, i.e., workers organizing to demand contract protection, state and local legislation, and changing public perception of workers' issues.

Our work is made more difficult because we do not have strong alliances, and on each of these four issues we cannot be victorious until we join with other people, placing our issues in the context of a larger struggle for justice. In each case, we have been given great opportunities for connecting with other people, but we have not met them because we have not had the political base that connects women, people of color, and workers within our own movement. One cannot create allies externally until alliances have been made internally. It should be noted that ENDA (the Employment Non-Discrimination Act) which was narrowly defeated by Congress in 1996, did not include transsexuals, despite their visible and extensive lobbying. In fact, some queer organizations actively lobbied *against* their inclusion on the grounds that we could never pass ENDA if they were included. It is urgent that we find ways to build and strengthen our political base both from within and without.

## A blueprint from the past

As we face the turn of the century, it is a good time to reflect on our past, our goals and strategies, and to make changes that help us overcome missed opportunities; that build on the good work we have done; and that lead us in alliance with others toward a broader vision of liberation.

I have found it helpful to look again at that defining moment in our history, the Stonewall uprising, to see what we can learn to help us think through the changes that have brought us from 1969's gay liberation, grounded in the politics of the left and social change, to the divisions we have today.

There is an ongoing debate about who was at Stonewall and what they did, all of which reflects our concern about race, class, and gender politics. In *Sexual Politics, Sexual Communities*, historian John D'Emilio reports his research:

> *On Friday, June 27, 1969, shortly before midnight, two detectives from Manhattan's Sixth Precinct set off with a few other officers to raid the Stonewall Inn, a gay bar on Christopher Street in the heart of Greenwich Village. They must have expected it to be a routine raid. New York was in the midst of a mayoral campaign— always a bad time for the city's homosexuals—and John Lindsay, the incumbent who had recently lost his party's primary, had reason to agree to a police cleanup. Moreover, a few weeks earlier the Sixth Precinct had received a new commanding officer who marked his entry into the position by initiating a series of raids on gay bars. The Stonewall Inn was an especially inviting target. Operating without a liquor license, reputed to have ties with organized crime, and offering scantily clad go-go boys as entertainment, it brought an "unruly" element to Sheridan Square, a busy Village intersection. Patrons of Stonewall tended to be young and non-white. Many were drag queens, and many came from the burgeoning ghetto of runaways living across town in the East Village.*
>
> *However, the customers at the Stonewall that night responded in any but the usual fashion. As the police released them one by one from inside the bar, a crowd accumulated on the street. Jeers and cat calls arose from the onlookers when a paddy wagon departed with the bartender, the Stonewall's bouncer, and three drag queens. A few minutes later, an officer attempted to steer the last of the patrons, a lesbian, through the*

*bystanders to a nearby patrol car. "She put up a struggle," the Village Voice reported, "from car to door to car again." At that moment,*

*"...the scene became explosive. Limp wrists were forgotten. Beer cans and bottles were heaved at the windows and a rain of coins descended on the cops....Almost by signal the crowd erupted into cobblestone and bottle heaving....From nowhere came an uprooted parking meter—used as a battering ram on the Stonewall door. I heard several cries of 'lets get some gas,' but the blaze of flame which soon appeared in the window of the Stonewall was still a shock." (Village Voice , July 3, 1969, p. 18)*

*Reinforcements rescued the shaken officers from the torched bar, but their work had barely started. Rioting continued far into the night, with Puerto Rican transvestites and young street people leading charges against rows of uniformed police officers and then withdrawing to regroup in Village alleys and side streets.*

*By the following night, graffiti calling for "Gay Power" had appeared along Christopher Street. Knots of young gays—effeminate, according to most reports— gathered on corners, angry and restless. Someone heaved a sack of wet garbage through the window of a patrol car. On nearby Waverly Place, a concrete block landed on the hood of another police car that was quickly surrounded by dozens of men, pounding on its doors and dancing on its hood. Helmeted officers from the tactical patrol force arrived on the scene and dispersed with swinging clubs an impromptu chorus line of gay men in the middle of a full kick. At the intersection of Greenwich Avenue and Christopher Street, several dozen queens screaming "Save Our Sister!" rushed a group of officers who were clubbing a young man and dragged him to safety. For the next few hours, trash fires blazed, bottles and stones flew through the air, and*

109

*cries of "Gay Power!" rang in the streets as the police, numbering over 400, did battle with a crowd estimated at more than 2,000.*

*After the second night of disturbances, the anger that had erupted into street fighting was channeled into intense discussion of what many had begun to memorialize as the first gay riot in history....The New York Mattachine Society hastily assembled a special riot edition of its newsletter that characterized the events, with camp humor, as "The Hairpin Drop Heard Round the World." It scarcely exaggerated. Before the end of July, women and men in New York had formed the Gay Liberation Front, a self-proclaimed revolutionary organization in the style of the New Left. Word of the Stonewall riot and GLF spread rapidly among the networks of young radicals scattered across the country, and within a year gay liberation groups had sprung into existence on college campuses and in cities around the nation. (pp. 231-233)*

The particulars of the Stonewall uprising provide the issues which, if tailored to the circumstances of the 1990s, could provide the core of a broad-based movement whose goal is justice and equality for everyone.

## Stonewall politics: then and now

What were the particular characteristics of Stonewall, and how do they compare with today's political environment?

• Stonewall happened in a vigorous political context, when there were rising expectations among oppressed groups, thanks to the great Civil Rights struggles, the growing anti-war movement, and the emergence of the second wave of the women's movement. Victories had been won.

• The economy was strong, and young people in particular were concerned about the conscience of the nation in terms of social policy. The new left had just demonstrated its strength and numbers in street battles with police at the Democratic National Convention in 1968. Dr. Martin Luther King, Jr. and Robert Kennedy had been assassinated, and anger over injustice had led to the burning of cities. All of these events, plus the atrocities of the Vietnam War, were brought directly into people's lives by television every night.

• Scattered across the country were homosexual organizations such as the Daughters of Bilitis and the Mattachine Society, and people who had been working to stop police harassment and raids on bars. They were poised to publicize and to organize this event to have far-reaching impact.

• This raid was one in a long history of harassment and imprisonment of queers; not only those who were out and visible, but especially those who crossed gender lines.

• Many of the primary players were transgendered people, lesbians, homeless youth, and people of color.

• A lesbian's resistance led others to gain the courage to resist also.

• The major tactics were direct action, organizing, and fun (cultural resistance and bonding through camp humor).

THERE ARE SOME stark differences between the political context of the late 1960s and that of the late 1990s. We are not in a time of rising expectations nor the ascendancy of the left. The greatest victories over the past decade have been those of the right. Here are a few of the changes that have taken place since the uprising at Stonewall:

• *Upward Redistribution of Wealth.* There is a wider gap between the rich and the poor than there has been since the turn of the century. Those who drive the country's economy and our work lives are for the most part invisible and unaccountable and their corporations and capital cross borders in search of greater profits for the few, at the expense of the many.

• *Economic Assault on Family and Community:* This global market economy has demanded worker mobility and created

111

a sense of transitory life, eliminating family, worksite, and community stability, continuity, and a sense of being rooted in people or place. Many people feel isolated and alienated, as well as stressed out from job insecurity and depleted community services. Lack of attachment to community (and each other), plus mis/disinformation has led voters to approve policies that destroy the tax base and civic infrastructure, leaving people to survive individually, if at all. Assaults against the welfare safety net, along with welfare-to-work programs designed to provide business low-paid or free labor, are increasing the number of poor families and decreasing workers' ability to organize.

• *Divided Allies:* The right has changed in its shape, constituency, visibility and power. It has become the prevailing voice of this moment. Working along economic and social fault lines, it has led people toward a church/corporate society that is producing an authoritarian ethic. With highly sophisticated media work and organizing, it has intensified the scapegoating of people of color, poor people, women, youth, trade unionists, and queers. We now either stand to be demolished in its path or organize together to create a resistance that saves us all. There is the sense that the left is in disarray, divided and ineffectual, and there is no context of victories for progressive people.

• *Growing Cynicism:* Virtually everyone in the country is cynical about electoral leadership and the functioning of government. While exacerbating this cynicism, the right organizes within this context to dismantle government programs that support human needs and work against injustice. It also promotes abandonment of civil liberties and an assault on the legal system. Indeed, many think its goal is to end democratic governance.

• *Prison/Industrial Complex:* Though, according to statistics, crime is now waning, we nevertheless continue to create a prison/industrial complex that is central to many states' economic development and is accompanied by privatized prison systems. Increasingly prisoner (free) labor is being used for private businesses, without accountability to voters. The issue of crime is a constant theme of politicians' campaigns and continues to be racialized.

• *A Pillaged Environment:* In the name of real estate development, economic growth, business interests, and tourism, the environment has been poisoned, demolished, polluted and destroyed, leaving many of us sick and sickened, wondering if there is still time to stop, and hopefully reverse, the damage.

• *Limited Access to Information:* A few major corporations control the media, and the media, in large part, control us—creating a massive consumer culture of people who do not have adequate social or political information to make critical judgments and informed decisions. In addition, the ideological bias of the media owners influences what and how news is reported.

• *Institutional Restructuring:* Institutions (schools, prisons, human services) are being privatized at a rapid rate; we are returning to states' rights; and people fear the separation of church and state will be disregarded as massive theocratic right organizations influence laws and take over institutions at the local level. The issues of school choice and vouchers allowing use of taxpayers' money to pay for religious school education are prime examples. (It should not be forgotten that many "religious" schools were established as a vehicle to allow white parents to remove their children from schools in predominately black and Hispanic communities.)

## Lessons from Stonewall

With such a changed political context, is there anything we can learn from Stonewall that could connect us to the vision of liberation we began with and fulfill that promise of change offered up by those who defended their dignity and humanity in front of a gay bar in 1969?

It seems to me that the issues represented by Stonewall are the central issues for today in this changed political environment: race, youth, poverty, and gender.

• *Race:* Queers of color at the Stonewall bar that famous

night were defending their dignity at a time when this country was in an intense struggle over race. Almost 30 years later, the country is still deeply conflicted about race. Virtually every social and economic issue is racialized—crime, drugs, welfare, public services, affirmative action, immigration, schools—and people of color are scapegoated as the cause of our problems.

Queers of color face multiple risks in a racist, homophobic, and sexist society, where economic injustice is rationalized as necessary and acceptable. Many of our lgbt? organizations have not supported the presence, politics, and the leadership of queers of color, nor have they taken many principled public positions on issues related to racial discrimination. Instead, more time has been spent trying to compare the struggles of queers to those of people of color.

The right has worked along fault lines of racism and homophobia to drive a wedge between communities of color and the queer community. This wedge has highlighted the failure of many in our movement to understand the connection among oppressions: how, for instance, the fate of queers of all races is inextricably connected to the elimination of racism. We have no experience that shows one oppression can be eliminated while others still exist. They are kindled by and thrive in the same culture of domination. As fascism in Germany rose on the backs of Jews, so can it grow here on the backs of people of color, and as Germany taught us, all marginalized groups soon are gathered into the scapegoating, the dehumanization, the demonization, the genocide.

Solidarity is the enemy of all oppressions. Divisions support them. Divisions within our queer movement will not be overcome nor solidarity achieved until white queers stop participating in white privilege and domination. To do so will require changing behavior and changing institutions: sharing power, focusing on issues that are not just queer specific, calling for vision and strategies and goals that do not support white privilege. Such a change will bring the idea of genuine, widespread social change to the discussion of participation in the military or the struggle for civil rights. It will also give us legitimate connection to other movements seeking justice and equality.

• *Youth:* "Patrons of Stonewall tended to be young and nonwhite....runaways....street youths." How many youth have run away from home, from school, from community because there was no place for them as queers? Because they were battered and abused or scared? What was true for many youth in the 1960s is true today: they can find little support for their lives as young queers or questioning people.

Youth played a critical role in the Civil Rights Movement and the Anti-War Movement of the 1960s and have had less participation in social justice movements since then. However, now in the queer movement, there are signs that youth are beginning to step forward to make demands and take leadership. They are in the forefront of new thinking about multi-issue, multi-racial, multi-gendered politics.

Schools are battlegrounds for the right. So much of their "cultural war" is waged over curricula, teachers' roles, parental rights, censorship, and privatization. Queer youth are on the front lines of these battles, often in isolation and without organizational support. In the name of family and community moral standards, the right fights against any mention of homosexuality in schools, whether in books, sex education classes, counseling sessions, or through the presence of openly queer youth and teachers. This enforced silence leaves our schools riddled with homophobia and provides no opportunities for young people to learn truths about queer lives and to have open discussions of their own sexuality.

What often stands in the way of adult queers supporting youth leadership, organizing, and issues is the terror brought about by the relentless demonizing of us as pedophiles, as people who sexually abuse children. As far as I can ascertain, we are the only oppressed group which is severed from its relationships with youth. Youth then experience the absence of adult mentoring, support, counseling, or befriending of both queer and nonqueer youth. Until we have this cross-generational connection, I

115

don't see how we can consider ourselves fully whole or fully human. We should confront the scapegoating accusation of pedophilia directly through internal and public education that places child sexual abuse in the larger context of understanding the ways adults (primarily heterosexual men) exert power over children for their own purposes. We must move boldly to be in supportive contact with queer youth wherever they are: in schools and universities, in homeless shelters and on the streets, in abusive or rejecting homes. To abandon them, as we often have in the past, makes all of our talk about freedom, justice, and equality ring false.

• *Poverty:* Of all the things dividing us in this country, the one that grows larger every day is the division of class. The separation intensifies as more money goes into the hands of shareholders and CEOs and less into the paychecks of workers, as jobs are eliminated or moved out of the country, as public assistance is decimated. One can anticipate even greater numbers of poor people as costs grow, salaries decrease and jobs disappear. It seems likely that the fight against economic injustice, here and internationally, will be the great struggle of the 21st century.

Many critics think that the failure to deal with class divisions and economic injustice is the primary reason our major social justice movements have not been entirely successful. Identity groups, such as women or people of color, have fought successfully for integration of some people into the mainstream but have not been successful in attacking the economic system which keeps great portions of their constituency in poverty.

Many lesbians and gay men have taken pride in asserting the upward mobility, wealth, and consumer potential of a portion of the queer population. They have used two deeply flawed economic surveys to point to the *value* of lesbians and gay men as community members because they have buying power. Invisible both to the eye of the mainstream lgbt? community as well as to heterosexuals are those large numbers of queers (especially youth and transgendered people) who live in precarious financial circumstances or in poverty.

116

I cannot see how a movement for gender liberation and human rights can be successful unless it addresses the deepest human needs of all of its constituents. To leave out economic justice as a goal is to leave out the primary concerns of those queers of color who experience racism built on economic injustice, lesbians who experience sexism associated with economic discrimination, transgendered people who battle prejudice in the job market, people living with AIDS and driven to poverty in the health care system, old queers, queers with disabilities, youth, etc. Ultimately, an unjust economic system affects all of us by creating a society that turns in on itself in the fight for survival: we live with gated suburbs and boarded up cities, people who go on cruises and people who cannot get a welfare check to buy food, and public services that have fallen away for everyone. The struggle for economic justice is our struggle.

• *Gender:* The people at Stonewall were seen as violating gender classifications of male and female through "inappropriate" dress and behavior: because they were drag queens, butch dykes, and queer. Thanks to the work of transgendered people, bisexuals, feminists, and youth activists, our understanding of the meaning of gender has grown enormously over the past decade. They have taught us that gender is possibly not biological but constructed, and that we have choice in the ways it is constructed. Moreover, they have led us to understand more thoroughly the connection between sexism and homophobia as gender oppression: that it is those who violate gender roles who are most severely punished, and that the enforcement of gender roles and designations is vital to the control of people, especially women, lesbians, gay men, transgendered, bisexual, questioning people, and ultimately, everyone.

Some of our writers on this issue, such as Martine Rothblatt in *Apartheid of Sex*, point out that binary designations of gender (male *or* female) dictate oppression because everything different from these designations must be seen as aberrant or wrong. Those who are different are thought of as gender outlaws or gender traitors. If there were no gender expectations, then why would it be thought wrong to be lesbian, gay, bisexual or transgendered, and why would women be considered a threat when we act as free humans rather than as people in restricted gender roles?

Work against gender classifications and gender oppression is at the revolutionary heart of our work. It is this work that promises to change the world by dismantling a primary structure of oppression and exploitation. It offers us a great opportunity to work as allies with heterosexual women and progressive men who are trying to eliminate gender restrictions. But first there is the work of alliance among lesbians, gay men, transgendered, transsexual, and bisexual people.

There are conversations and controversy throughout our community about issues relating to transgenderism and transsexuality, to gender identity and gender behavior, and to sexual identity and sexual practice. For example, when I wrote the first edition of *Homophobia: A Weapon of Sexism,* many of us had common assumptions about the definition of "lesbian." Now, we are just as likely to be uncertain about exactly who and what a lesbian is. People wonder, for instance, about what is currently called the "JoAnn Loulan question:" can one be a lesbian and sleep with a man? And what about lesbians who sleep with their gay male friends? Or there's the transsexual question: can one be born a male, transition through hormones and surgery to femaleness, and be a lesbian? What about those who lived their lives successfully as men with the attendant male privilege before making this change? On the other hand, can one be born a woman, transition through hormones and surgery to maleness, and be a lesbian? Or can women or men who have had no hormones or surgery identify themselves as the "other" gender? Can one be a female bisexual and relate to both genders and be part of the "lesbian community?" What do butch and femme have to do with lesbian sex, life, or liberation? Is one identity more "lesbian" than the other? Is there an actual lesbian identity, true above all others?

These questions, and others like them, are met with

considerable excitement by some and resistance and anger by others. There is conflict about the acceptance of bisexuals and transsexuals into lesbian and gay organizations. There is limited understanding of transsexuality, and there is conflict based in class privilege between those who can afford hormones and operations, and those who fight to maintain a psychiatric designation of "gender identity disorder" in order to qualify for insurance to pay for these procedures.

THE CURRENT DISCUSSION of sexual and gender identity makes me think about core issues. I still believe, as I did in 1988 when I wrote *Homophobia: A Weapon of Sexism*, that the central issue is sexism. Homophobia has worked very effectively to keep women and men frightened of stepping out of the gender roles and identities that imprison us. And these are the roles that underpin male power and control.

We must take that structure down. It has been the fuel behind the theocratic right's attack on us for the past two decades. When they say that lesbians and gay men are a major threat to the family and to moral structures, they are actually saying we are a major threat to male power. We are a threat to a hierarchy that places men "over" women and children in a system that then has to consider women and children inferior in a way that can lead to psychological and/or physical violence. An examination of the rhetoric from Focus on the Family or Promise Keepers shows that their litany, in one way or another, is male hierarchy, male dominance—all in the guise of Christian belief and "traditional families."

Hierarchy and domination have everything to do with who has power and control over our bodies and how we use them. For now, sexism and homophobia stand in the way of our having the full ownership of our bodies. We still live in a society that says it is wrong for a woman to love a woman or to have sex with a woman. For all of us to be free, we have to change the world so that it is good to love anyone; that sex is positive, no matter what gender is involved; and that we have choice

119

concerning the use of our bodies, as long as we do not use them to harm others. As long as sexism (which demands male control of our bodies) exists, I do not believe we will ever eliminate homophobia.

There is a strong progressive lesbian feminist politic that recognizes that gender fluidity and transgenderism will help bring about changes in the rigid gender rules that restrain us. It also acknowledges that bisexuality and transsexuality touch the heart of our belief that all of us must have control of our bodies—we must own them. That is why we support reproductive choice, work to end sexual assault, and fight for all of us to be able to love and have sex with the person we choose.

The question that lies at the heart of this matter is not that of gender identity but that of who supports male power and privilege. Whatever forms our gender and sexual identity take, ever-changing or static, we have to find ways to rebel against roles designed to keep us under control or to exert control over others. This takes more than gender bending or cross-dressing or accentuating butch/femme or having surgical procedures or having sex with both women and men or being an out lesbian— it takes resistance to virtually everything the culture has taught us. It takes subversion and outright refusal. Most of all, it takes a commitment to liberation and freedom for all of us.

We have the hard work before us of moving from early ideas of sexual liberation and more recent themes of civil rights to the more comprehensive, deep-rooted gender liberation. This requires discussion of gender fluidity and ambiguity as well as concepts of power and equality when gender restrictions are not the norm. As gender liberationists dismantling power, we can work toward a goal of freedom for women, queers and, ultimately, men everywhere.

## A choice of direction

As I look at our work of almost a decade since *Homophobia: A Weapon of Sexism* was written, I am quite amazed by its variety, especially at the local level where queers have engaged their communities in discussions and actions which have made the world a safer place for queers to be. On the national level, organizations such as the Black Leadership Forum and the National Gay and Lesbian Task Force embrace multi-issued, multi-racial politics. Yet, too often within queer organizing, advocacy, education, electoral, and media campaigns, the leadership is white and middle-class, adept at passing, and the issues are those that the leadership feels most poignantly. The overwhelming focus has often seemed to be one of getting our place at the table of the status quo. Some of us have thought that when the right attacks us, we can get acceptance by being more like the right, or at the very least, by being more like the middle America that drifts rightward rather thoughtlessly in a time when tough critical thinking needs to be done.

Though often we have managed to do successful public education about who some of us are, we have yet to establish the many alliances we need to create a successful major movement. I believe this is a time of opportunity because we are poised to enter into a different kind of relationship with other people who experience injustice. We have put some of our issues out, and now is the time to link those issues with others, making ideological and personal connections. Queer people suffer because of homophobia/heterosexism, racism, sexism, and economic injustice, as well as oppression based on religion, age, and physical ability. When we do not acknowledge those issues within the lives of our constituency, we fail to treat our own people as whole and as having equal worth. To be free in a free society we have to integrate these issues and fight together on many fronts—for all of us.

To work for freedom, for justice and equality, calls forth a critical question: is our goal to finds ways to fit into and be accepted by a society that is currently increasing economic injustice, scapegoating people of color and women, passing laws to control queers, polluting the environment, etc.? Or is our goal to work for a transformed society that honors all of its members, respects and treasures their differences, and offers them, with fairness and equality, opportunity for prosperity and happiness? Our people are divided today. I believe our work is to bring them together in all the many ways we can work for a world that is livable for everyone.

# Annotated Bibliography

Anzaldua, Gloria & Moraga, Cherrie, eds. 1983. *This Bridge Called My Back: Writings by Radical Women of Color*. New York: Kitchen Table: Women of Color Press.

This classic collection of essays, stories, and poems is the benchmark for our understanding of feminism as defined by women of color.

Berlet, Chip, ed. 1995. *Eyes Right! Challenging the Right Wing Backlash*. Boston: South End Press.

Leading community activists, researchers, and organizers discuss the right wing movements that are at work to destroy the gains of the New Deal and the Civil Rights Movement.

Bornstein, Kate. 1994. *Sexual Outlaw*. London: Rutledge Press.

This autobiographical book provides a humorous and mostly feminist analysis of a transsexual life and transgender issues.

Cleaver, Richard & Myers, Patricia, eds. *A Certain Terror: Heterosexism, Violence & Change*. 1993. Chicago: The Great Lakes Regional Office, American Friends Service Committee.

This anthology provides a lively look at the interconnectedness of heterosexism, racism, sexism, class oppression and militarism and offers vision and strategies for making change.

D'Emilio, John. 1983. *Sexual Politics, Sexual Communities: The Making of a Homosexual Minority in the United States, 1940-1970*. Chicago: University of Chicago Press.

Through unearthing the early work of homosexual groups and placing them in a political context, this book connects the current queer movement to its origins.

Feinberg, Leslie. 1996. *Transgender Warriors: Making History from Joan of Arc to RuPaul*. Boston: Beacon Press.

This combination of historical and personal narrative about the lives of transgendered people links gender and class oppression and calls for a wider understanding of justice and freedom.

Heron, Ann, ed. 1994. *Two Teenagers in Twenty*. Boston: Alyson Publications.

Young people from around the country discuss issues such as coming out, trying to pass as straight, friends, running away, incest, religious concerns, and making initial contact with the gay community. Includes bibliography and pen pal service.

Hutchins, Loraine & Kaahumanu, Lani eds. 1991. *Bi Any Other Name*. Boston, Alyson Publications.

Over 70 men and women talk about their lives as bisexuals who have experienced and fought prejudice from both gay and straight communities and now share their stories in the process of forming a new bisexual community.

Kahn, Karen. 1995. *Front Line Feminism, 1975-1995: Essays from Sojourner's First 20 Years*. San Francisco: Aunt Lute Books.

Over 100 essays are organized around the topics of identity, economic injustice, politics of family, reproductive freedom, women's health, sex and sexuality, violence against women, and alliance building.

Lorde, Audre. 1984. *Sister Outsider*. Trumansburg, New York: The Crossing Press.

This classic collection of essays and speeches by a Black lesbian feminist provides the leading edge of contemporary analysis of the connections among the oppressions and the development of feminist multi-racial and multi-issue politics.

Pharr, Suzanne. 1996. *In the Time of the Right: Reflections on Liberation*. Berkeley: Chardon Press.

Divided into four sections, this book describes the domination politics of economic injustice, racism, sexism and homophobia; the rise of the right and its multi-issued agenda; the way homophobia and racism divide us; and offers strategies for building a world that provides equality and justice.

Rofes, Eric. "Gay Issues, Schools, and the Right-wing Backlash." *Rethinking Schools: An Urban Educational Journal*, Spring 1997, Vol. 11, No. 3, p 1, 4-5.

This article provides an analysis of attacks against queer youth and gay issues in schools, organizing efforts in response to these attacks, and the need for making schools safe for lesbian, gay, bisexual, and transgendered youth and the teachers committed to serving all their students.

Rofes, Eric. 1995. *Reviving the Tribe: Regenerating Gay Men's Sexuality and Culture in the Ongoing Epidemic.* New York: Harrington Park Press.

In a thoughtful and piercing examination the lives of gay men within the ongoing AIDS epidemic, this book addresses directly the impact on mental health and the spirit, the need to reclaim sexuality and gay male identity, and the ways authentic community can be regenerated and built.

Rothblatt, Martine. 1995. *The Apartheid of Sex: A Manifesto on the Freedom of Gender.* New York: Crown Publishers.

Declaring it unnecessary for the state to require binary (male/female) classification of sex, this book calls for a revolutionary change in our understanding of sex and gender that will dismantle old systems of power and offer the possibility of freedom for all of us.

Segrest, Mab. 1994. *Memoir of a Race Traitor.* Boston: South End Press.

A personal and political journey of a white Southern lesbian feminist into the heart of race politics and struggle, this book offers a vision of possibility for the social change that committed activism can bring.

Smith, Barbara. 1983. *Home Girls: A Black Feminist Anthology.* New York: Kitchen Table: Women of Color Press.

The personal stories, essays, and poems in this classic collection detail a Black feminist politic that emerges from a sense of home, of place in the Black community, and leads us to understand the necessity of a political analysis that supports wholeness and connection.

Vaid, Urvashi. 1995. *Virtual Equality: The Mainstreaming of Gay & Lesbian Liberation.* New York: Anchor Books.

This book provides an analysis of efforts to bring lesbians and gay men into acceptance by the heterosexual mainstream and the subsequent failure to do the hard and often risky work that would bring true liberation.

# 2nd Edition Acknowledgements

My heartfelt thanks to my friends Mandy Carter, Reneé DeLapp, Jean Hardisty, Kerry Lobel, Judy Matsuoka, Beth Richie, and Eric Rofes who found time within their own social justice work to give this afterword a critical reading. I am also thankful to my friend and editor, Deborah Dudley, who brought patience and generous ideas to this writing.

Suzanne Pharr
Portland, Oregon
*June 1997*

\* \* \* \* \*

The Women's Project would like to thank the following funding organizations for their partial funding of both the original and expanded editions of *Homophobia: A Weapon of Sexism*:

The Astraea Foundation
Haymarket People's Fund
The Gill Foundation
National Community Funds

# THE WOMEN'S PROJECT

All proceeds from the sale of this book and *In the Time of the Right: Reflections on Liberation* go directly to the Women's Project to support its work to eliminate sexism and racism. Since 1981 that work has been guided by the following mission:

> Our goal is social change, or as the poet Adrienne Rich writes, "the transformation of the world."
>
> We take risks in our work; we take unpopular stands. We work for all women and against all forms of discrimination and oppression. We believe that we cannot work for all women and against sexism unless we also work against racism, classism, ageism, anti-Semitism, ableism, heterosexism, and homophobia. We see the connection among these oppressions as the context for violence against women in this society.
>
> We are concerned, in particular, about issues of importance to traditionally under-represented women: poor women, aged women, women of color, teenage mothers, lesbians, women with disabilities, women in prisons, etc. All are women who experience discrimination and violence in their lives.
>
> We are committed to working multi-culturally, multi-racially, and to making our work and cultural events accessible to low-income women. We believe that women will not know equality until they know economic justice.
>
> We believe that a few women working in coalition and consensus with other women can make a significant change in the quality of life for all women.

# About Chardon Press

Founded in 1988, Chardon Press publishes books and other materials relating to or funding the work of social justice and social change.

## FUNDRAISING

■ **Fundraising for Social Change, Third Edition**
by Kim Klein (1995)

■ **Grassroots Grants: An Activist's Guide to Proposal Writing**
by Andy Robinson (1996)

■ **Grassroots Fundraising Journal**
(6 issues annually; Special editions: Board of Directors, Getting Major Gifts)

To order the above or for more information on other Chardon publications contact:

**CHARDON PRESS**
**PO BOX 11607**
**BERKELEY, CA 94712**
phone: (510)704-8714
fax: (510)649-7913
E-mail: chardn@aol.com

## GENERAL INTEREST

■ **In the Time of the Right: Reflections on Liberation**
by Suzanne Pharr (1996)
**To order call (501) 372-5113**

■ **Volver a Vivir/ Return to Life**
PROJIMO/Suzanne Levine, ed. (1996)
**To order call (415) 387-0617**

■ **The Family Guide to the Point Reyes Peninsula**
by Karen Gray (1996)
**To order call (415) 663-9114**

■ **Naming Our Truth: Stories of Loretto Women**
by Ann Patrick Ware, ed. (1995)
**To order call (502) 865-5811**

■ **Home on the Range: Recipes from the Point Reyes Community**
Foreword by Ed Brown (1988)
**To order call (415) 663-1075**